READY TO LEARN

P9-APB-209

Third Grade
Workbook

Table of Contents

READY TO LEARN

Third Grade

A NOTE TO PARENTS, CAREGIVERS, AND TEACHERS

The *Ready to Learn* series is an excellent tool for assisting your child, grandchild, or student in developing readiness skills in mathematics, reading, and writing during their early learning years. The colorful and engaging workbooks, workpads, and flash cards support the acquisition of foundational skills that all children need to be successful in school and everyday life.

The *Ready to Learn* series develops skills targeted to the Common Core State Standards. The practice workbooks include explanations, strategies, and practice opportunities that engage your young learner with the building blocks needed to become a confident mathematician, reader, and writer. The workpads provide additional practice for the key concepts addressed in the workbooks, and the flash cards support fluency in basic math and reading concepts.

Ready to Learn workbooks include an overview page to inform adults of the learning objectives inside, as well as a certificate at the end of each section to present to your child or student upon completion of the workbook. It is recommended that you display each certificate earned in a prominent location where your child or student can proudly share that he or she is excited to be a learner!

While the *Ready to Learn* series is designed to support your child's or student's acquisition of foundational skills, it is important that you practice these skills beyond the series. You can do this by having your child or student find examples of what he or she has learned in various environments, such as letters and words on menus at a restaurant, numbers at a grocery store, and colors and shapes on the playground.

Thank you for caring about your child's or student's education.
Happy learning!

 # Reading

Table of Contents

Third Grade Reading Readiness

Third grade reading requires kids to think deeply about what they read and be able to communicate what they have read in greater detail. Students read longer text from a variety of genres and formats with a greater focus put on writing about what they've read to help kids make connections with their meanings, lessons, and ideas. Support and enable your child or student to follow his or her interests when choosing books or other reading materials. Let his or her natural curiosity fuel a desire to read.

Vocabulary

Sight Words

These sight words will be frequently seen in third grade. Practice them until you can recognize and read them when you see them.

about	fall	kind	pick
better	far	laugh	shall
bring	full	light	show
carry	got	long	small
clean	grow	much	start
done	hold	myself	today
draw	hot	never	together
drink	hurt	only	try
eight	keep	own	warm

5

Practicing Sight Words

Roll a die and write the sight word that matches the number you rolled in the correct column below. Roll until you fill the grid.

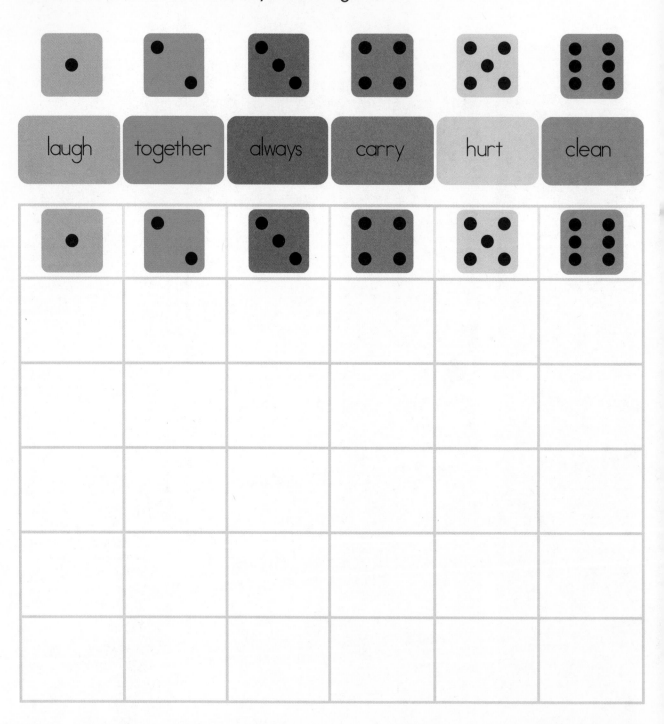

laugh	together	always	carry	hurt	clean

Which word filled the chart first? Write a sentence using that word on the line below.

_____

_____

Vocabulary

Syllables

A syllable is a word or part of a word that is heard when you make one clap.

Example:

1 syllable	2 syllables	3 syllables
bear	li/on	el/e/phant

Read the words below out loud as you clap each syllable. How many syllables do you hear? Sort the words into the correct categories based on the number of claps you hear. Write them on the lines below.

wolf   pelican   monkey   snake   kangaroo   whale
porcupine   turtle   giraffe   octopus   walrus   seal

1 SYLLABLE	2 SYLLABLES	3 SYLLABLES

Decoding New Words

If you are not certain how to read a word, it may help you to figure out the word's syllables, or chunks. A helpful hint is to remember that there will usually be at least one vowel (A, E, I, O, U, and sometimes Y) in each syllable in a word.

Example: dif/ 🖐 /fer/ 🖐 /ent 🖐

Break these words into syllables based on the vowels in each chunk and write how many syllables each word has on the line across from each word. Use a colored pencil to show the division of the words.

h o l/i/d a y   __3__ syllables

s n o w m a n   _____ syllables

h a l l w a y   _____ syllables

g a r d e n   _____ syllables

t o g e t h e r   _____ syllables

w i n t e r   _____ syllables

s k a t i n g   _____ syllables

e x p e r i m e n t   _____ syllables

e x c i t e d   _____ syllables

s c i e n t i s t   _____ syllables

Vocabulary

Using Context Clues

Sometimes using the other words in a sentence can help you figure out the meaning of a word in the sentence that you do not know or understand.

Example: I packed the apples in my bag, but I excluded some because they had bruises on them.

Excluded means separated or taken away, so some of the apples didn't go into the bag because they had bruises on them.

Read each sentence below. What does each word in red mean? Underline the words in the sentence that help you figure out the meaning of that word. Write your own definition of the word on the lines below each sentence.

I ate too much candy, and now my stomach feels queasy.

_____

_____

I saw a gigantic giraffe at the zoo. It was as tall as a tree!

_____

_____

We built a tower so high that it wobbled, and then it toppled over.

_____

_____

I was sneezing, so my dad gave me a handkerchief for my nose.

_____

_____

Nothing scares my little brother because he is so adventurous.

_____

_____

We are so eager to go to the birthday party on Friday night!

_____

_____

Vocabulary

Using a Dictionary

Looking a word up in the dictionary can help you understand what the word means. The words in a dictionary are alphabetized. That means they are in alphabetical order. Each page has guide words at the top that tell you what words are included on that particular page.

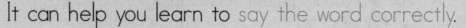

HOW CAN A DICTIONARY HELP YOU?

It can help you see how to spell a word.

It can help you learn to say the word correctly.

It can help you find out the meaning of a word based on parts of speech (e.g., noun, verb, adjective).

It can help you find out how many syllables are in a word.

It can help you find synonyms and antonyms for a word.

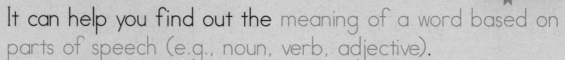

Look up the words below in a dictionary. Write a sentence based on the definition you read in the dictionary on the lines below.

carnivore
_____
_____
_____

invent
_____
_____
_____

magnify
_____
_____
_____

volunteer
_____
_____
_____

Reading Comprehension

Following Directions

Follow the directions below to complete the neighborhood map.

1. Draw an American flag on a pole in front of the post office.
2. Draw your house in the southeast corner of the map.
3. Draw two children beside the school.
4. Draw a fire truck inside of the fire station.
5. Draw a car on Main Street driving toward the gas station.
6. Draw a librarian at the library holding a book.
7. Draw yourself on Orange Street near your house.

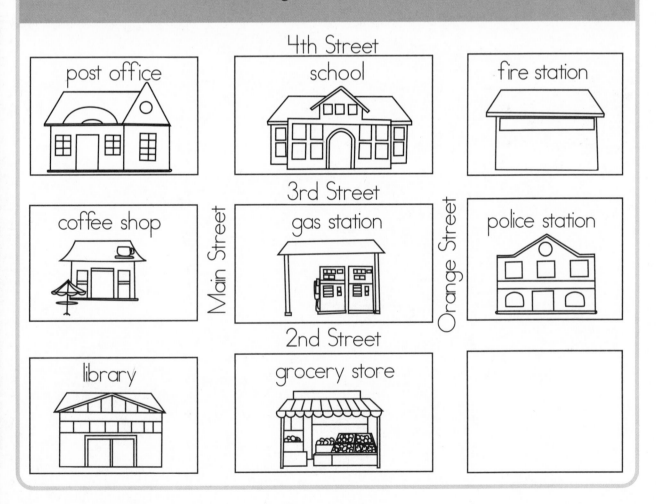

Reading Comprehension

Following Directions

Procedural writing **teaches us** how to follow directions by moving step-by-step through the directions until the task is complete.

Follow the directions below to make a delicious s'more!

HOW TO MAKE A S'MORE AT HOME WITH A MICROWAVE

You will need:

- 1 milk-chocolate bar
- 1 marshmallow
- 1 graham cracker
- a microwave-safe plate
- a microwave

Make sure you have an adult's permission first!

1. Place a graham cracker square on the plate.
2. Break off two pieces of chocolate from the chocolate bar and place them on top of the graham cracker.
3. Place another graham cracker square on the same plate next to the first graham cracker square.
4. Place a marshmallow on top of the second graham cracker.
5. Put the plate in the microwave and cook for twenty seconds.
6. Carefully take the plate out and place the graham cracker with the marshmallow on top of the graham cracker with the chocolate so that the marshmallow is touching the chocolate.
7. Enjoy!

Following Directions

Answer the questions about making your s'more. Write your answers on the lines below.

How many pieces of chocolate did you use?

_____

_____

Did you put the s'more in the microwave or the oven?

_____

_____

How many marshmallows did you use?

_____

_____

What kind of crackers did you use for your s'more?

_____

_____

What was the first step in making your s'more?

_____

_____

How long did you cook your s'more?

_____

_____

How did your s'more taste?

_____

_____

Sequencing

Sequencing is putting directions in the correct order.
You can sequence the order of any activity.

Read the steps for building a snowman below. Write the numbers in the boxes to put the steps in order and then rewrite the steps in the correct order on the lines below.

Give your snowman a hat and scarf. ☐

Roll one small, one medium, and one large snowball. ☐

Put a stick on each side of the medium snowball for arms. ☐

Place the small snowball on top of the medium snowball. ☐

Put a mouth, button eyes, and a carrot nose on the small snowball. ☐

Place the medium snowball on top of the large snowball. ☐

1. _____

2. _____

3. _____

4. _____

5. _____

6. _____

Sequencing

You can also sequence the order of a story that you read.

Read the passage below and find out what happened in the beginning, middle, and end of the story.

Gail's Girls

Gail has three little girls. They love to bake! They always help Gail make wonderful cakes and cupcakes at home. First, they help her take out all the ingredients. Then they help Gail mix the ingredients in a big bowl. They love to lick the spoon after mixing! After the cakes and cupcakes are finished, they all have a tea party in the backyard.

Answer the questions about the story. Write your answers on the lines below.

What did Gail's girls help her do?

_____

_____

What do they help her do first?

_____

_____

What do they help her do next?

_____

_____

What do they love to do after mixing the ingredients?

_____

_____

What do they do last?

_____

_____

Compare and Contrast

When we compare and contrast things, we tell how they are alike and how they are different.

A great way to compare and contrast things is to use a Venn diagram.

A Venn diagram is made of two large overlapping circles. Each side of the circles tells how things are different. The middle tells how they are alike.

Think about what you know about elephants and giraffes. Write in the Venn diagram about how they are alike and how they are different.

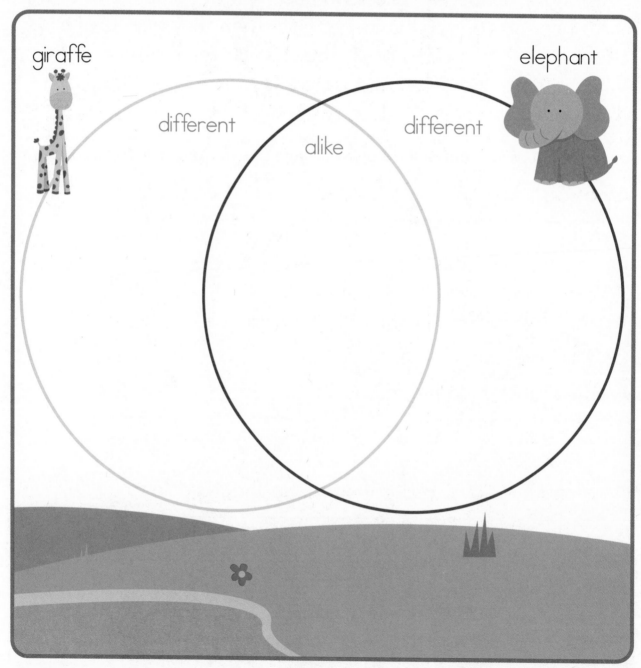

Compare and Contrast

Read the passage below and compare and contrast the characters in the story.

Maddy and Lucy Go Camping

Maddy and Lucy love to go camping. Every time their mom and dad tell them they are planning a trip to the lake, they squeal with delight. For Maddy, it means time to swim and read quietly under a tree. For Lucy, it means time for board games and water skiing. Maddy loves all the camping food. Her favorite foods are hot dogs and roasted marshmallows. Lucy likes to bring healthier food from home. She eats raw carrots and granola bars when they go camping. While Maddy and Lucy both love to go camping for different reasons, they are both sad to leave the lake every time one of their camping trips comes to an end.

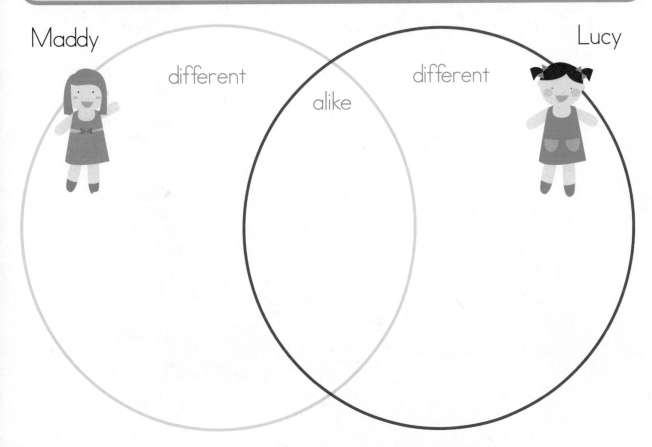

Maddy

Lucy

different   alike   different

Reading Comprehension

Facts and Opinions

A fact is something that can be proven with evidence.

An opinion is something that is a personal belief.

Example: It is a fact that there are fifty states in the United States.

In my opinion, strawberry is the best flavor of ice cream.

Read each sentence below and determine if it is a fact or an opinion.
Circle the correct answer.

Two nickels equal a dime.	fact	opinion
Dogs are better pets than cats.	fact	opinion
Chicago is a city in Illinois.	fact	opinion
The American flag is red, white, and blue.	fact	opinion
My mom makes the best chocolate-chip cookies.	fact	opinion
Kids should be able to choose their own bedtime.	fact	opinion
Four quarters equal one dollar.	fact	opinion
Thanksgiving is everyone's favorite holiday.	fact	opinion
A blue whale is the largest whale.	fact	opinion
Everyone loves to go swimming.	fact	opinion
It is fun to ride a roller coaster.	fact	opinion
There are twelve months in a year.	fact	opinion

Facts and Opinions

Facts can be proven by reading about the subject, looking it up online, or asking a parent or teacher. Opinions can mean that one person may believe something while another may disagree.

Read the sentences below and write the word fact or opinion beside each sentence.

Our family should have a dog.	
The cafeteria should serve French fries every day.	
Everyone loves to go camping.	
Ten dimes equal one dollar.	
The city of Portland is in Oregon.	

Write two sentences that are facts.

_____

_____

_____

Write two sentences that are your opinions.

_____

_____

_____

Reading Comprehension

Main Idea

The main idea is what the story is mainly about.

Example: A book titled *Tammy's First Bus Ride*
            is probably about a bus ride.
            That is the main idea.

Read the passage.

> Anthony and Rebecca love to travel. They have flown to many different countries around the world and have loved every one of them. Their favorite country to visit was Spain, but they also loved France and Japan.

Circle the main idea.

- Anthony and Rebecca's favorite country is Spain.
- Anthony and Rebecca have traveled to France.
- Anthony and Rebecca enjoy traveling around the world.

> Barry and Marion rode their bikes to the grocery store. They bought all of their favorite candy and snacks. Barry likes chocolate, and Marion likes pretzels. They decided to share their treats. Marion discovered that she likes chocolate, and Barry found out that he likes pretzels!

Circle the main idea.

- Marion likes pretzels.
- Barry and Marion rode their bikes to the grocery store.
- Barry and Marion tried new snacks and liked them.

Reading Comprehension

Main Idea and Supporting Details

Look for the main idea and supporting details as you read the passage below.

Earth Day

Today is Earth Day. Our class is learning about recycling. Recycling means taking something that has been thrown away and making something new out of it. Recycling is good for the planet because recycling and reusing things means we are throwing away less garbage. We are reusing bottles in class today by making planters out of the used water bottles. I chose a yellow flower to put in my new planter. I like Earth Day.

What is the main idea of this passage?

_____

_____

What are some of the supporting details in the passage?

_____

_____

_____

What was made from the recycled water bottles?

_____

_____

_____

Reading Comprehension

Making Predictions

Making a prediction means thinking about what you are reading and making a guess about what might happen next. Clues in the text and things you already know can help you predict what might happen next.

Read the sentences below and circle what you predict comes next.

I got my lunch and walked to the cafeteria table, but my shoelace was untied, and I...

a. ate my lunch.   b. tripped and fell   c. sat with a friend.

After staying up late last night, I feel really...

a. tired.   b. happy.   c. hungry.

I left the gate open in our backyard, and our dog...

a. ate his dinner.   b. ran out to chase a cat.   c. played fetch with me.

If you don't brush your teeth, you might...

a. get to eat candy.   b. get a cavity.   c. feel full.

We left late for the movie, and we...

a. got extra popcorn.   b. saw the movie on time.   c. missed the beginning.

I took my umbrella outside today because...

a. it was snowing.   b. it was sunny.   c. it was raining.

Reading Comprehension

Making Predictions

Good readers make predictions before, during, and even after reading a story. They look at the cover of a book and the title, and try to predict what the story might be about before beginning to read. While reading, good readers stop every once in a while to think about what might happen next and use clues from the story to help make predictions. Finally, good readers often think about how the story might continue after the author's ending.

Read the passage below and make predictions as you read.

Road Trip

We all piled in the car for a long road trip. We were finally going to visit our cousins who live on a dairy farm in Wisconsin! It was going to be a very long day and night in the car with my brother, Nathan. He is younger than me. He likes to copy everything I say and do, and sometimes it gets on my nerves. My mom packed all sorts of games and activities for us to play along the way. She said she wants us to be good, look at the beautiful scenery, and enjoy the road trip. Wisconsin, here we come!

Answer the questions about the passage. Write your answers on the lines below.

What do you think is going to happen after the kids arrive at their cousins' house?

_____

_____

_____

_____

What clues are there in the passage to support your prediction?

_____

_____

_____

_____

Reading Comprehension

Fiction

Some stories are realistic fiction, which means even though the story is made up, it could happen in real life.

There are also fairy tales, which often have imaginary characters like wizards and dragons.

Fiction stories can also be fables, which are fictional stories with a lesson or moral. Fables often have animals as the main characters.

Read the passage below and circle what kind of fiction it is.

The Little Red Hen

The little red hen was a very hard worker. She cleaned the farm, cooked the food, and took care of her chicks. One day, she found a grain of wheat. "Who will help me plant this wheat?" she asked.

"Not I," replied the dog, duck, cat, and pig.
So she planted it herself.
After the seed grew and the wheat was harvested and ground into flour, the little red hen asked, "Who will help me bake the bread?"

"Not I," replied the dog, duck, cat, and pig.
So she baked the bread herself.
When the bread was baked, she and her chicks began to eat.

"May we have some bread?" asked the dog, duck, cat, and pig.

"No, you may not!" said the little red hen. "I did all the work myself! My chicks and I will eat the bread."

From then on, the dog, duck, cat, and pig tried to be more helpful to the little red hen and their other friends.

a. realistic fiction
b. fairy tale
c. fable

Fiction

Look at the book titles below and draw a line to the correct type of fiction.

Nonfiction

Nonfiction reading can explain, inform, and persuade. The nonfiction information shared must be based on factual information, which means the information can be proven to be true.

Biographies are true stories about a real person's life.

Informational text provide facts about people, places, things, and events. Sometimes this type of nonfiction text will give information about a person's job, such as a farmer or doctor.

When someone writes a letter and shares true information, it is nonfiction text.

Read the passage below and answer the question.

> Dear Nana,
>
> I miss you a lot! I wish I could come visit you, but right now I have to stay home because it is not our family vacation time.
>
> What have you been doing to stay busy? I have been doing a lot of things! Two of my favorites are learning to ride a horse and playing board games.
>
> The horse I am riding is named Blaze because he has a white streak on his forehead. He is very gentle to ride. I love when he gallops!
>
> I have been playing a lot of board games almost every day. My favorite games are word games. I love trying to spell words I know, and I have even learned a few new ones. Maybe we can play some games when I finally get to visit you!
>
> Love,
> Eila

What is some true information that Eila shared with her grandmother in her letter?

_____

_____

Nonfiction

Look at the book titles below and draw a line to the correct type of nonfiction.

informational text

biography

Using the Cover to Make Predictions

The cover of a book can help you predict what is inside.

Creatures
of the Sea

Written By Amelia Hunter
Illustrated By M. L. Rose

What is the title of the book?

Does it give you a clue?

What is the picture on the cover?

What clues does the picture give you?

Use the cover to help you answer the questions. Write your answers on the lines below.

What do you predict this book will be about?

_____
_____
_____
_____
_____

What clues on the cover did you use to make your prediction?

_____
_____
_____
_____
_____

Book Covers

Book covers can help you predict what a book is about. They can give you clues to what kind of book it will be.

Take a look at the book covers below and write a complete sentence telling a friend what you think the book is about.

Harry Houdini Master of Magic

_____

_____

_____

_____

_____

_____

Hockey Basics

_____

_____

_____

_____

_____

How to Make Brownies

_____

_____

_____

_____

_____

LEARN HOW TO TELL JOKES

_____

_____

_____

_____

_____

Book Covers

Design your own book cover. Make sure that the title and illustration give the reader clues about your book. Don't forget to include an author and illustrator.

Table of Contents

The **table of contents** **tells you** what information can be found in a book **and** what page it begins on.

Read the table of contents below.

Dolphins

Table of Contents

Use the table of contents above to help you answer the questions. Write your answers on the lines below.

How many chapters are in the book?

What chapter can be found on page 10?

If you think dolphins are found around the world, what chapter will help you find out if that is true?

To find out what dolphins eat, what page would you turn to?

Index

The index is at the end of the book. Some books have them, and others don't. It is a list of all the topics that are in the book and all the pages where the topics are located. The words or phrases listed in the index are in alphabetical order.

Read the index below.

INDEX

Babies 6–7

Food 2–3, 9

Habitat 4–5

Predators 8, 10–11

Use the index above to help you answer the questions. Write your answers on the lines below.

On what pages can you find information about dolphins' habitats?

_____

_____

On what pages can you find information about dolphin food?

_____

_____

What topic can be found on pages 8, 10, and 11?

_____

_____

If you wanted to find out about dolphin babies, what page or pages should you turn to?

_____

_____

Glossary

Some books have a list of words on a certain page or in the back of the book called a glossary. A glossary is like a little dictionary. It gives the meanings of important words from the book. The words in the glossary are in alphabetical order.

Take a look at the glossary below and find the information needed to answer the questions.

GLOSSARY

Blowhole — The hole on top of a dolphin's head that it uses to breathe air

Intelligent — The ability to think deeply

Mammal — A warm-blooded animal that breathes air and typically has live babies

Pod — A group of dolphins that lives and travels together

Predator — An animal that eats other animals for food

What is a group of dolphins called?

_____

_____

What does the word "mammal" mean?

_____

_____

What does a dolphin use its blowhole for?

_____

_____

Diagrams

Diagrams **often** provide details beyond the textual information **shared in** nonfiction text.

Read this paragraph and study the diagram.

Cone-shaped volcanos are the most common type of volcano. A volcano may erupt from its crater or from a secondary vent. The side of a cone-shaped volcano is called the **flank**. Layers of ash and lava build up on the flank over time due to multiple eruptions. The more eruptions there are, the bigger the mountain will become. When **magma** travels upward and comes out of the crater, it is called **lava**.

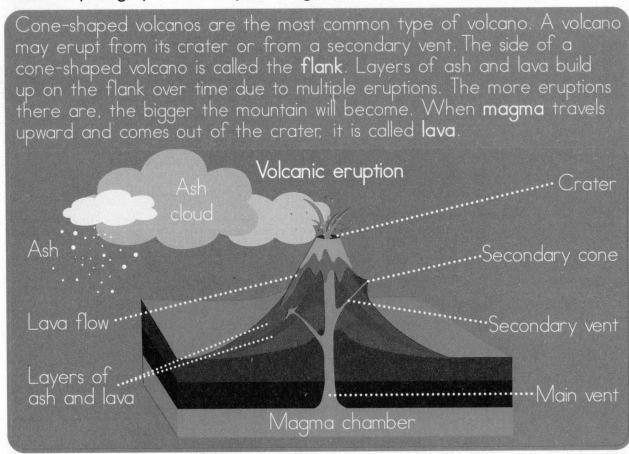

Volcanic eruption

Answer the questions on the lines below. Check the box to share where you found the answer to each question.

What is the area called where a secondary vent reaches the surface of a volcano?

_____

_____

Did you answer this question by: ☐ reading the text? ☐ studying the diagram?

Why does a volcano's flank get bigger over time?

_____

_____

Did you answer this question by: ☐ reading the text? ☐ studying the diagram?

What falls from an ash cloud?

_____

_____

Did you answer this question by: ☐ reading the text? ☐ studying the diagram?

Bold Print, Maps, and Graphs

There are a variety of other text features in books that help readers comprehend what they are reading.

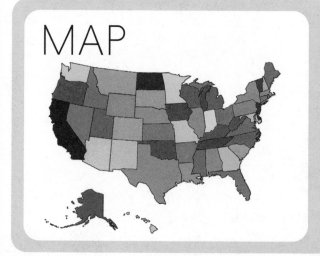

MAP

Maps are often in nonfiction books to show readers where something is located. A map will be labeled and have a key to explain what the map is representing.

BOLD PRINT

Dolphins are **intelligent** creatures. They speak to each other with squeals and squeaks. They are **mammals** that breathe air through a **blowhole**.

Bold print means that some of the words in the book are **bigger or darker than others**. This usually means the word or phrase is important. Sometimes bold print words and phrases are part of a glossary that tells you what they mean.

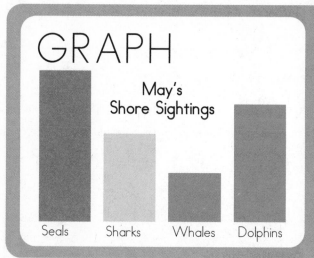

GRAPH

May's Shore Sightings

Seals · Sharks · Whales · Dolphins

A graph is a kind of chart that provides data and supports what the text is saying. It is labeled and will have a title that explains what the information in the graph is about.

Informational Text

Informational text **is written to** inform **or** explain something. **Read the passage below and visualize (picture in your mind) what you are reading.**

An Amazing Animal

The octopus is one of the world's most amazing animals. Their eight arms, big eyes, and beak make them unique. Their ability to change colors and blend into their surroundings makes them interesting to watch.

There are over 300 different species of octopuses. They range in size from small enough to fit on the tip of a person's finger to the size of a living room! The giant Pacific octopus is the biggest octopus and is about 16 feet long. The smallest is the star-sucker pygmy octopus. It is less than 1 inch long.

Octopuses have eight arms with suction cups on them for grabbing things. They have two gills and, amazingly, three hearts! Because an octopus does not have bones, it can fit through tiny spaces. An adult giant Pacific octopus can squeeze through a hole the size of the top of a soda can!

Most octopuses live on the sea floor and eat creatures like shellfish, shrimp, and fish. They move along the ocean floor using two of their arms to "walk" and the other six to search for food. When an octopus needs to get away quickly, it shoots out a jet of water using its powerful muscles and zooms away backward.

Nonfiction Text

Comprehending Informational Text

Answer the questions about the informational text "An Amazing Animal." Write your answers on the lines below.

What are four facts you learned about octopuses?
_____
_____
_____
_____
_____
_____
_____
_____
_____
_____

What can an octopus do if it needs to get away quickly?
_____
_____
_____
_____
_____
_____

What is the name of the biggest species of octopus?
_____
_____

What is the name of the smallest species of octopus?
_____
_____

Reading Informational Text

Read the passage below and visualize what you are reading.

River Otters

Playful and fun, the river otter is a mammal that lives throughout North America. They live in lakes, rivers, streams, and ponds. Anywhere there is water, river otters seem to be comfortable finding a home.

River otters like to live in groups, but the females give birth in one den area, while the males live in a different section of the den. Instead of building their own dens, they often use fallen trees or old beaver dams as their den. They line it with leaves, grass, and moss to keep them comfortable.

Otters love to play together. They are often seen sliding down slippery hills on their bellies. They are also known to belly flop into the water and play fight with their friends.

Otters like to eat together too. Groups of otters, called a "raft" when in the water, can be seen floating on their backs and using their bellies as tables for their food. They are great hunters and can stay underwater up to four minutes at a time while searching for food. Their favorite food is fish, but they also like to eat crayfish, frogs, toads, and even snakes!

Nonfiction Text

Comprehending Informational Text

Answer the questions about the informational text "River Otters." Write your answers on the lines below.

What are three facts you learned about river otters?

What do you know about otters' dens?

What is a group of swimming river otters called?

How are river otters playful?

Reading Biographies

Biographies **are nonfiction** stories about important or famous people's lives. It is informational text because it teaches you facts and allows you to make connections to the person's life. Read the biography below and think while you read.

Terry Fox

When Terry Fox was twenty-two years old, he inspired the whole world by setting out on his Marathon of Hope. He ran across Canada to raise money for cancer research. This was amazing because Terry had lost most of his right leg to cancer four years earlier. He ran on a prosthetic leg!

After a run when he was seventeen, Terry's knee hurt so much that he went to see a doctor. The doctor discovered it was more than just sore from running; Terry had cancer.

The doctor told Terry that to save his life, a team of doctors would have to remove most of his right leg. After the surgery, he had to take medication that made him feel very sick most of the time. He received the medicine at a clinic where there were lots of other cancer patients. Terry wished he could help them all. So Terry came up with the idea for his Marathon of Hope.

In April of 1980, he began his run in St. John's, Newfoundland, Canada. As he ran across the country, people started lining the streets to wish him luck and make donations. After 143 days, Terry made it all the way to Thunder Bay, Ontario. He ran over 3,338 miles! Terry was a real-life hero!

Nonfiction Text

Comprehending Biographies

Answer the questions about the biography "Terry Fox."
Write your answers on the lines below.

What are three facts you learned about Terry Fox?

_____

_____

_____

_____

_____

_____

_____

What gave Terry the idea to run his Marathon of Hope?

_____

_____

_____

_____

_____

_____

_____

_____

What did the doctors have to do to save Terry's life?

_____

_____

_____

_____

How many years passed between Terry's news that he had
cancer to when he ran his Marathon of Hope?

_____

_____

_____

Reading Persuasive Text

Persuasive text involves an author using his or her words to persuade others to either change their thinking or do something based on the author's opinion, which includes reasons and supporting facts.

Read Marcia's persuasive letter to her parents. Be sure to think about her reasons and supporting facts as she tries to persuade them to let her have a cell phone.

Dear Mom and Dad,

It's almost my birthday. I am excited to be turning ten years old! I have been on Earth now for a decade, and I think I am old enough to have my own cell phone.

Although you may think I am still too young, having a cell phone is important for someone my age. A cell phone in my pocket will help us keep in contact because we can text each other. You might want to ask me, "Are you almost done visiting with Sandra?"

I can text back and tell you, "We are still painting."

You can then tell me what time to be home: "We are having dinner at 5 p.m., so be home by 4:45."

A cell phone is also great to have for taking photos of the special memories in our family life. I can create albums on my phone and show them to Grandma and Grandpa when we visit them next summer. I promise to ask permission before I send any photos to my friends. I will also show you any photos that are sent to me.

Whenever you want to know where I am, you can track me using an app on your phone. Vicky's parents do that with her all the time, and it makes her parents feel better knowing where she is at all times. I think you would feel better knowing where I am too.

I will only turn ten years old one time. Getting a cell phone for my birthday this year will make it the best birthday ever!

Love,

Marcia

Comprehending Persuasive Text

Answer the questions about the persuasive letter Marcia wrote her parents. Write your answers on the lines below in complete sentences.

What does Marcia want to be given for her tenth birthday?

_____

_____

_____

_____

Marcia gave her opinion for why she thinks she should get a cell phone for her birthday. What are two of her reasons? Be sure to include her supporting details in your answer.

_____

_____

_____

_____

_____

_____

_____

_____

_____

_____

What do you think Marcia's mom and dad will decide to do? Why do you think that?

_____

_____

_____

_____

Fictional Text

Mixing Real Life and Imagination

When an author writes realistic fiction, he or she uses people and events that could be real but uses his or her imagination because the people and events in the story or passage did not really happen in the author's life.

Read the realistic fiction passage below.

Josh's Super Sandwich

As he rolled to the edge of his bed, Josh struggled to open his eyes. "Wow, it's still dark out," he mumbled. He rolled over to look at his brother, Randall, on the bottom bunk. He was still sound asleep.

Josh quietly tiptoed down the hall and into the bathroom. He was happy he was able to take a shower before his older sister. After he got dressed, he walked downstairs. "Everyone is still asleep," he said, "but I need to pack my lunch for school!"

As he opened the refrigerator door, he whispered, "Master chef Josh will now make a supersonic, triple-decker ham and cheese sandwich!" Josh started taking things out of the fridge. Once the counter was covered with his needed ingredients, he looked at all of his options and decided to start with a buttered toast slice. Then he created a triple stack of ham, cheese, ham, cheese, ham, and cheese. He then topped his stack with a tomato slice, lettuce leaf, and a second buttered toast slice.

Holding up the plate to look closely at his layered creation, Josh exclaimed, "This is the best sandwich I have ever made!"

As he began to pack up his sandwich, he finally heard the sound of footsteps coming down the stairs and said, "Oh my! I wonder if I am going to have to share?"

Fictional Text

Comprehending Realistic Fiction

Answer the questions about the realistic fiction passage "Josh's Super Sandwich." Write your answers on the lines below using complete sentences.

What are two things Josh did before making his super sandwich?

_____

_____

_____

_____

Why do you think Josh called his sandwich a "supersonic, triple-decker" sandwich? Support your reasoning using text from the passage.

_____

_____

_____

_____

If you could create a super sandwich, what ingredients would you use?

_____

_____

_____

_____

Draw a picture of your super sandwich below. Be sure to label each of its layers!

Fictional Text

When an author writes fictional stories or passages from his or her imagination, he or she often uses animals that can talk and events that may not happen in real life.

Read the fictional passage below and think while you read.

Claire the Clumsy Cow

Claire cruised across the pasture looking for something to do. It was nearly milking time, and she wanted to avoid going back to the barn. As she got to the far end of the field, she saw the fence was broken and she realized she could walk through it! Claire had gotten her nickname, Claire the Clumsy Cow, because she was always tripping over things and falling down.

Claire clip-clopped along the road. After walking for a while, she saw something she had never seen before: a fast-flowing river. Claire had never seen so much water moving so quickly. She moved slowly down to the water's edge and tried to take a drink, but she couldn't reach the water. She decided to put her front hooves over the edge and right into the water, but she still couldn't reach down far enough. As she edged forward, she started to slip. With a loud splash, she fell right in!

Now she had all the water she could drink, but she was focusing on the fact that she was floating. She said, "I am not afraid. I am enjoying floating in this stream."

After a little while, she remembered it was time for dinner, and she was getting hungry. Claire made her way back to shore and pulled herself up onto the bank. She clip-clopped back to the farm and walked right up to the milking barn. Mr. Farmer said, "Hi, Claire the Clumsy Cow! Where have you been?"

"I went for a swim," replied Claire, "and I had so much fun! From now on, you can call me Claire the Buoyant Bovine*!"

*Buoyant means to float, and bovine means cow.

Comprehending Fictional Text

Answer the questions about the fiction passage "Claire the Clumsy Cow."
Write your answers on the lines below in complete sentences.

Why was Claire called Claire the Clumsy Cow?

_____

_____

_____

_____

What was the problem that led to Claire falling into the stream?

_____

_____

_____

_____

What did Claire say that let you know she enjoyed the water?

_____

_____

_____

_____

What does Claire mean when she called herself a "buoyant bovine"?
Use text from the passage to support your reasoning.

_____

_____

_____

_____

Did you make a personal connection to this passage? Think of a
time when you were clumsy like Claire.

_____

_____

_____

_____

Myths

Myths are traditional, often ancient, stories with supernatural beings, heroes, and kings that serve as a way to explain natural occurrences and human behaviors.

Read a famous Greek myth that parents told their children to explain a human behavior. Think about what the behavior might be as you are reading.

Midas and His Golden Touch

King Midas was a very wealthy king. He loved two things more than anything: gold and his precious daughter, Marigold.

Every day King Midas would spend hours and hours staring at his gold treasures. But he was never quite satisfied. When he and Marigold enjoyed a meal together, he would often say to her, "I would be even happier if I could have even more gold."

One day, as King Midas was locking his treasury room after visiting his treasures, he saw a stranger walking toward him wearing a flowing red cloak. The stranger came very close to the king and whispered in his ear, "I see you are a rich king."

"Yes, I have a treasury filled with gold coins, trinkets, and treasures," remarked King Midas, "but it is not enough for me!"

"Why?" inquired the elderly stranger. "You have more wealth than all of the kings in this land!"

He explained to the hunched man, "If every building in my kingdom was made of pure gold, I would still want more! I wish that everything I touched turned to gold!"

The stranger winked at the king. A bony finger came out from behind the cloak and touched King Midas's shoulder while he said, "If a golden touch is what you want, then a golden touch is what I will give." He paused for a moment and then whispered in King Midas's ear again, "Be careful what you wish for..."

When King Midas turned to thank the stranger, he was gone. The king wondered if what had happened was just a dream.

The next morning, King Midas jumped out of bed and grabbed a chair to steady himself. The chair instantly turned to gold! His eyes became as big as saucers, and he quickly touched everything he could see in his room, including his bed, a side table, and a tall dresser. "Gold, gold, gold, and more gold!" he cheerfully exclaimed.

He began to put on his kingly clothes, which instantly turned to gold. King Midas announced to his guard, "I could not be any happier!" With great excitement he walked out to his garden courtyard. He saw many of his beautiful roses were in full bloom. He went from rose bush to rose bush and touched each flower until every rose had transformed into pure gold.

Suddenly, King Midas's stomach began to growl. He walked from the courtyard into his dining room, where he summoned his servants to bring him breakfast. When he lifted his goblet to drink, both the cup and juice within turned to gold. When he used his now golden silverware to bring a slice of meat to his mouth, the meat turned to gold when it touched his lips! "How will I be able to eat anything?" asked the king.

King Midas then heard a whimpering sound coming from the courtyard. He recognized the voice and knew it was his beloved Marigold. He hurried back to the courtyard.

"What is wrong, my precious Marigold?" inquired the king.

"Oh, Papa," Marigold sobbed, "I am fine, but what is wrong with our garden? I came here to pick you a beautiful bouquet of colorful roses, but all the flowers have turned to gold and have no fragrance."

King Midas, sad to see Marigold so unhappy, said, "Please don't cry, my child," as he bent down and kissed her on the forehead. "Don't you feel better now, knowing that I love you more than any rose in this garden?"

Marigold did not answer. King Midas stepped back, shocked. He realized his kiss had turned Marigold into a golden statue! He cried out, "Oh no! What have I done?"

Out of the corner of his eye, he caught a glimpse of something red moving toward him. It was the elderly stranger who had met him outside his treasury room the day before. The stranger whispered in King Midas's ear, "My king, how do you like your golden touch now?"

"I am so very unhappy," moaned King Midas. "I realize gold will never truly make me happy! I would rather be the poorest man in the world than never hear Marigold call me 'Papa' again!"

"You are now much wiser than you once were, King Midas," said the stranger. "Go and dip yourself into the river that runs by your castle. The water will take away your golden touch." He pulled a clay object from beneath his cloak and handed it to the king. "Then fill this pitcher with river water and sprinkle it on all you have touched."

King Midas bowed low to thank the stranger, but when he lifted his head, the stranger was gone.

The king ran as fast as he could and jumped into the river. His clothes instantly turned back into fabric. He was overjoyed! He quickly filled the pitcher with water and returned to the courtyard. He poured some of the water onto Marigold's golden figure. Her cheeks became rosy, and she gazed lovingly at her father. "Thank you, Papa!" she cried. "I could hear you, but I could not talk or move."

King Midas took his daughter into his arms, kissed her, and hugged her tightly. "Now I am truly happy in my heart, for I now know what is most important. You mean more to me, Marigold, than all the gold in the entire world!"

Comprehending a Greek Myth

Answer the questions about the Greek myth "Midas and His Golden Touch." Write your answers in complete sentences on the lines below. Be sure you use text from the story to aid in answering the questions.

Who are the three characters in this story?

_____

_____

_____

_____

_____

_____

_____

_____

What are the five settings for this story?

_____

_____

_____

_____

_____

_____

_____

_____

_____

_____

_____

_____

_____

_____

_____

Fictional Text

Analyzing a Greek Myth

You were asked to think about what parents were trying to teach their children when reading the "Midas and His Golden Touch" myth. Which moral best matches the myth? Check one of the four boxes below and then use text from the myth to justify the reasoning for your choice on the lines. Write your response using complete sentences.

☐ It is important to be kind to everyone because then others will be kind to you.

☐ Do not be greedy because it can cause problems in your life.

☐ Always be honest because people will believe you if you are wrongly blamed.

☐ Listen to the advice of older people because their wisdom can help you make good decisions.

_____

_____

_____

_____

_____

_____

_____

_____

_____

_____

Fictional Text

Analyzing a Greek Myth

If you think about who is telling a story, such as a myth, when you are reading it, then you are trying to figure out who is the narrator. The narrator can be a character in the story or can be a voice who is not a character in the story, but can explain to readers what is happening and how characters are thinking and feeling.

Who is the narrator of this story? Check one of the four boxes and then use text from the myth to justify the reasoning for your choice on the lines below.

☐ King Midas   ☐ A Narrator Voice

☐ Marigold   ☐ Stranger

_____

_____

_____

_____

_____

_____

_____

_____

Draw an illustration of what the stranger looked like in your mind when you were reading the myth. Then list the words, phrases, and/or sentences that inspired your stranger drawing.

Reading Fables

Fables are short stories that teach a lesson or moral. They often have animals as the main characters.

Read the fable below and think about the main characters as you read.

The Lion and the Mouse

Lion lay asleep in the forest, his great head resting on his paws. Mouse, a tiny timid creature, came upon the furry beast unexpectedly and in her fright and haste to get away, she ran across Lion's nose! Awakened from his nap, Lion laid his huge paw angrily on Mouse's tail.

"Spare me!" begged poor Mouse. "Please let me go, and one day I will surely repay you and your kindness."

Lion was quite amused to think that Mouse could ever help him. After he thought about his choices for a while, though Lion finally decided to let Mouse go.

Later in the year, while stalking his prey in the forest, Lion was caught in the ropes of a hunter's net. Unable to free himself, he filled the forest with his angry roar. Mouse recognized the gruff voice and quickly found Lion struggling in the net. Running to one of the main ropes that bound him, Mouse gnawed on the fibers until the rope broke and Lion was free.

"You did not believe me when I said I would repay you someday," said Mouse. "Your kindness meant so much to me, and I am thankful that I was able to repay you today."

Comprehending Fables

Answer the questions about the fable "The Lion and the Mouse."
Write your answers on the lines in complete sentences.

Which moral best matches the fable? Check one box and then write your
reasoning on the lines below.

☐ Never, ever give up.

☐ Do to others as you want them to do to you.

☐ There is always a way to figure something out.

_____

_____

_____

_____

What word do you think best describes Mouse's personality? What actions and
dialogue in the fable support your reasoning?

_____

_____

_____

_____

_____

_____

_____

_____

_____

Opinion Text

Reading Opinion Text

A writer shares his or her thoughts or beliefs and supports his or her viewpoint with detailed reasons.

Read the story below and think about the author's viewpoints as you read.

The Cleanup Crew

When you have to do chores by yourself, it can take forever! That is why it is much better to do chores with someone you know.

My mom and grandma make dinner, so my sister and I are in charge of cleaning up. For a long time, Sarah and I would take turns to clean the kitchen every other night. By the time I was done, it was almost bedtime! She said it was the same for her too.

Why does it take so long to clean the kitchen? Because there are a lot of things that need to get done. The chore to clear the table takes four steps. You have to put away the food that is still on the table, including the salt and pepper shakers, butter, and milk. Then you need to carefully carry all the dishes and silverware to the sink and get them ready to put in the dishwasher. After that, you have to wrap up the leftovers and put them in the fridge. Lastly, you need to take a damp cloth and wipe down the tabletop and counters.

The other chore is sweeping the floor and giving our dogs, Peanut and Popcorn, fresh water. This chore also takes four steps. To sweep the floor, you need to move the chairs away from the table and sweep underneath. Next, you need to sweep around the bottom of the counters and use a dustpan to gather up the crumbs and throw them into the trash can. The last thing to do is clean the water bowl, fill it with fresh water, and put it back on the floor on the dog bowl mat.

One day, I had an idea, and I shared it with Sarah. "We can work together each night and be done in half the time!" I told her that since we have two jobs that both take four steps, if we each do one job every night, it will take half the time and we can play before we go to bed every night of the week.

That's when we became the cleanup crew, and now we know that working together as a team is terrific!

Opinion Text

Comprehending Opinion Text

Answer the questions about the opinion passage "The Cleanup Crew."

Write your answers on the lines below in complete sentences.

What is the author's opinion on cleaning up after dinner?

What are the details for doing the table cleaning chore?

What are the details for completing the floor and dog bowl cleaning chore?

Which of the two chores would you prefer to do and why?

Reading Opinion Text

Read the passage below and think as you read.

Chocolate or Regular Milk?

I have wondered which I really like better, chocolate milk or regular milk. Because I can see the milk when I drink it, the only way I can know for sure is to drink a glass of each kind with a blindfold over my eyes!

To make my taste test fair, I poured the same amount of cold chocolate milk and regular milk into two separate glasses. Since I like to eat a peanut butter and banana sandwich with milk, I made this kind of sandwich, put it on a plate, and cut it into two triangles.

Before I began my taste test, I asked my dad to help me. I gave him a table I created to help me collect my data. I told him I would use the numbers one to ten. One means I do not like something, and ten means I *really* like something. Then I put on a blindfold and made sure my mouth was not covered up. Lastly, my dad placed the two glasses of milk on the table in front of me so I would not know which one was which when I tasted the milk flavors.

I tasted each type of milk without looking. As my dad named each testing category, I told him my number for each glass of milk.

After I finished all of the testing and added up the score for each type of milk, I have come to the conclusion that chocolate milk is my favorite!

Tested Categories	Regular Milk	Chocolate Milk
Taste Bud Reaction	7	10
Creamy Texture	10	9
Flavor with Sandwich	9	9
Total Score	26	28

Comprehending Opinion Text

Answer the questions about the opinion passage "Chocolate or Regular Milk?"
Write your answers on the lines below in complete sentences.

How did the author make sure his milk-tasting test would be fair?

_____
_____
_____
_____

What does the author like about chocolate milk? Look for
supporting details in the table to help you answer the question.

_____
_____
_____
_____

Look at the table in the passage. In which category did the
author like regular milk the same as chocolate milk?

_____
_____
_____
_____

What is your opinion on regular milk versus chocolate milk? Do not
forget to include details in your answer to support your reasoning.

_____
_____
_____
_____
_____
_____

Reading a Letter

Writing a letter to a friend or family member is also a form of nonfiction text.

Read the letter below and think about what is being shared while you are reading the letter.

Dear Mom and Dad,

    I'm having a great time at summer camp. I've had so much fun here already!

    When you dropped me off the first day, I was very upset. I didn't know why you thought I'd like to spend my summer at some place in the woods. But it didn't take me long to realize how much fun camp can be!

    The four other guys in my cabin, Jack, Bill, Ned, and Steve, are great! Jason, our cabin leader, showed us to our cabin on the first day. We all got to choose our bunks. I share a bunk with Jack. We helped each other unpack and make our beds. Then we headed down to the dock for a swim. After dinner, there was a campfire and sing-along.

    Today we woke up early and had a delicious pancake breakfast. After that we went on a hike through the forest. In the afternoon we headed back to the lake to canoe. We all had to keep our life jackets on. Jason would swim under the water and jump up and surprise us. It was hilarious! He said we are getting ready to go on a river adventure on Saturday. I'm really looking forward to that day!

    I'm really glad I came after all. I know I'm going to have a great summer here at Camp Crystal Lake!

Love,

Andy

Comprehending a Letter

Answer the questions about the letter Andy wrote to his parents. Write your answers on the lines below.

Where was Andy when he wrote the letter?

_____

_____

_____

_____

Write two things Andy told his parents about camp life.

_____

_____

_____

_____

Why do you believe Andy's opinion of camp changed?

_____

_____

_____

_____

Who are three people you would like to write a letter to, and why?

_____

_____

_____

_____

_____

Reading a Rhyming Poem

Poetry **can** make you aware of the author's feelings **and** paint a picture in your mind.

Read the poem below and visualize while you read.

The Blindfold

1. I am wearing a blindfold,
   Ready to do what I am told.
   And since I cannot see,
   Will something be given to me?

2. Will I be told to touch or eat?
   Either way, I hope it's a treat.
   A basketball would be fun to dribble,
   Or a cupcake would be fun to nibble.

3. What is this I have been given?
   If feels soft. Maybe it's a mitten.
   I hear a sound, but I'm not sure.
   I think it might be a gentle purr.

4. What do you think is in my hand?
   Something small or something grand?
   The only way I'll know for sure
   Is to remove the blindfold—that's the cure!

Comprehending a Rhyming Poem

Answer the questions about "The Blindfold."

Write your answers on the lines below in complete sentences.

How did this poem make you feel as you were reading about what the boy was experiencing?

_____

_____

_____

_____

_____

_____

_____

_____

_____

_____

A poem's structure is made of stanzas. A stanza is a group of lines that form a small thought or topic within a poem. Sometimes a stanza is called a verse.

What number is your favorite stanza in "The Blindfold," and why is it your favorite?

_____

_____

_____

_____

_____

_____

_____

_____

Posters

Reading and Comprehending Posters

Just like a story, when a poster is made, the author has designed it for a purpose.

Authors sometimes design posters to provide information.

Authors also design posters to make the information easy to read and understand. Posters often have big, bold print and illustrations.

Look at the posters below. What is the message or information the author wants you to know? Write your answers on the lines below.

What does the author want the reader to know?

_____

_____

What is the important information on this poster?

_____

_____

_____

_____

What does the author want the reader to know?

_____

_____

What is the important information on this poster?

_____

_____

_____

_____

Posters

Design Your Own Poster

What will be the purpose of your poster? Think about what pictures and words you want on your poster. What information do you want the reader to know?

Draw your poster in the box below.

Keep Reading!

Remember, good readers read every day! Choose any book you like, find a comfortable place, and start reading.

Fill out the reading log below for every book you read.

Independent Reading Log

Book Title	Did you enjoy the book?	Fiction or Nonfiction? Explain how you know.
	👍 👎	
	👍 👎	
	👍 👎	
	👍 👎	

Independent Reading Log

Keep Reading!

Fill out the reading log below for every book you read.

Independent Reading Log

Book Title	Did you enjoy the book?	Fiction or Nonfiction? Explain how you know.
	👍 👎	
	👍 👎	
	👍 👎	
	👍 👎	

CERTIFICATE
of Achievement

....

has succesfully completed
3rd Grade Reading

Signed:

....

Date:

....

Writing

Table of Contents

Third Grade Writing Readiness

In third grade, children grow as writers as they write more structured and complex pieces. More focus is given to planning, revising, and editing personal and peer's work to learn more about the writing process. A great way to incorporate writing at home is to write a collaborative story. Begin a story and have your child write the next paragraph. Then take turns back and forth to add details and events to the story. Besides creative story writing and writing poetry, children and students need experience in writing nonfiction texts, such as information about people, places, things, and events. If possible, have your child or student write stories, poems, and nonfiction text using a computer or tablet.

Cursive Writing

Cursive writing is a more fluid way to write letters and words. The more you practice, the better you'll get. Once you have mastered the way to write in a loop style, it will be a much faster way to write!

To practice, begin on this page. You will find that the letters are not in alphabetical order on the following pages. Instead, they are grouped so you can practice joining letters together to form words.

Note: You do not have to do all of the activities in this book in cursive.

a   *d*   *c*   *o*   *t*

First trace and then practice writing the cursive letters and words on the lines below.

a   *a*   *a*

d   *d*   *d*

c   *c*   *c*

o   *o*   *o*

t   *t*   *t*

dad   *cat*   *coat*

Practicing Cursive Writing

a e n p f v

First trace and then practice writing the cursive letters and words on the lines below.

a a a

e e e

n n n

p p p

f f f

v v v

fan van

pen pan

Practicing Cursive Writing

u e i q d l

First trace and then practice writing the cursive letters and words on the lines below.

u   u   u

e   e   e

i   i   i

q   q   q

d   d   d

l   l   l

liquid

quill

73

r k s m a g

First trace and then practice writing the cursive letters and words on the lines below.

r   r   r

k   k   k

s   s   s

m   m   m

a   a   a

g   g   g

mask

grass

Practicing Cursive Writing

u s o b h j

First trace and then practice writing the cursive letters and words on the lines below.

u   u   u

s   s   s

o   o   o

b   b   b

h   h   h

j   j   j

job   bush

blush   sob

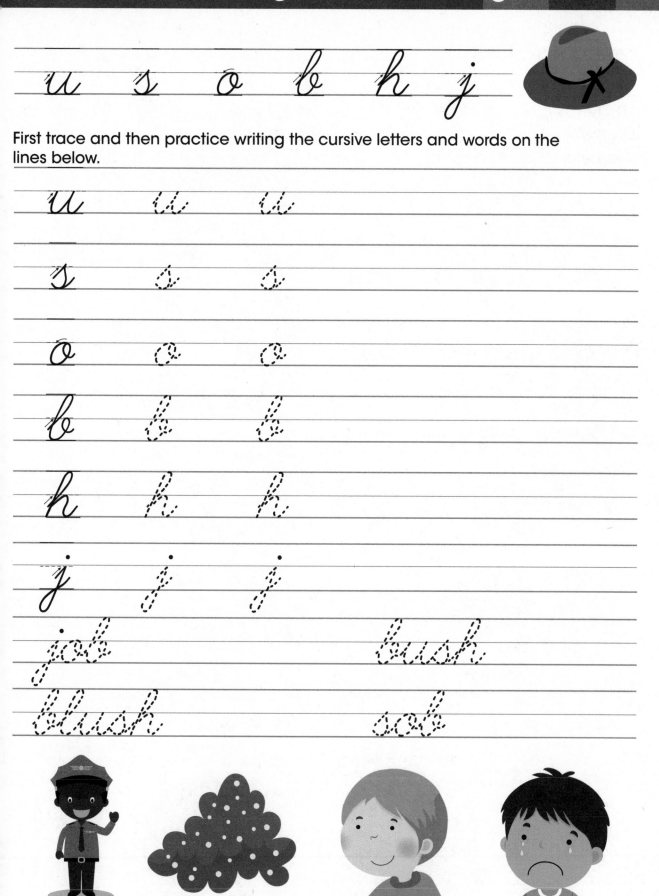

75

Practicing Cursive Writing

z o y x w

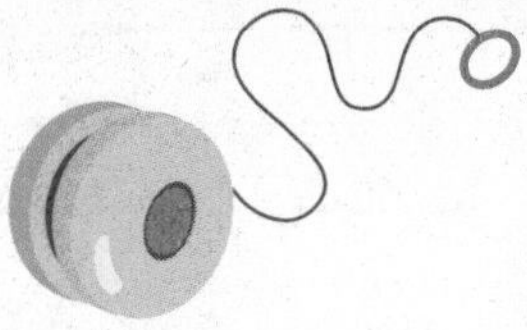

First trace and then practice writing the cursive letters and words on the lines below.

z z z

o o o

y y y

x x x

w w w

yo-yo

zoo

ox two

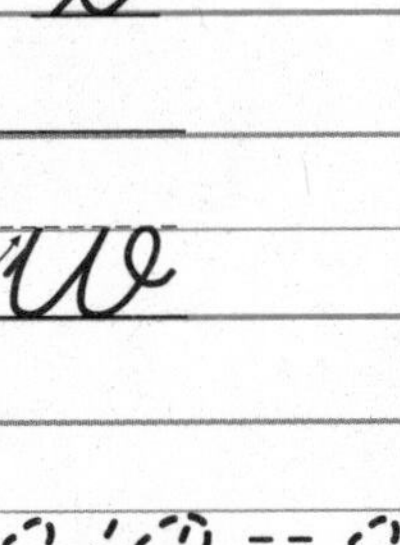

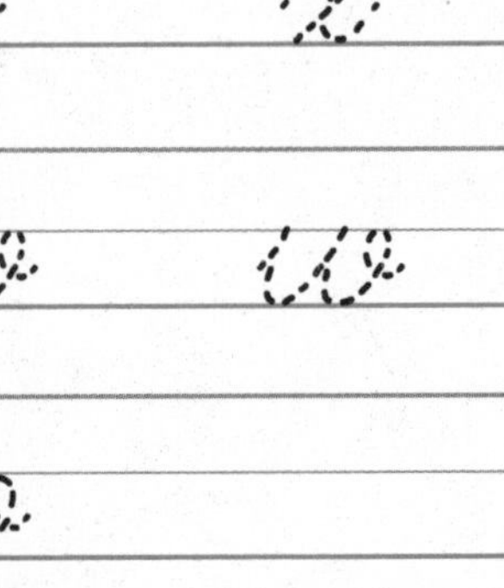

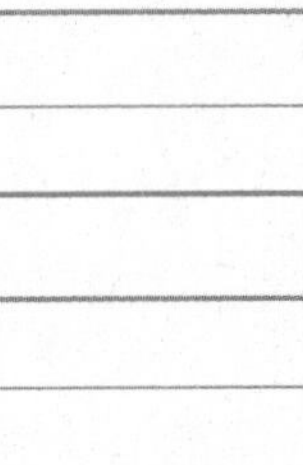

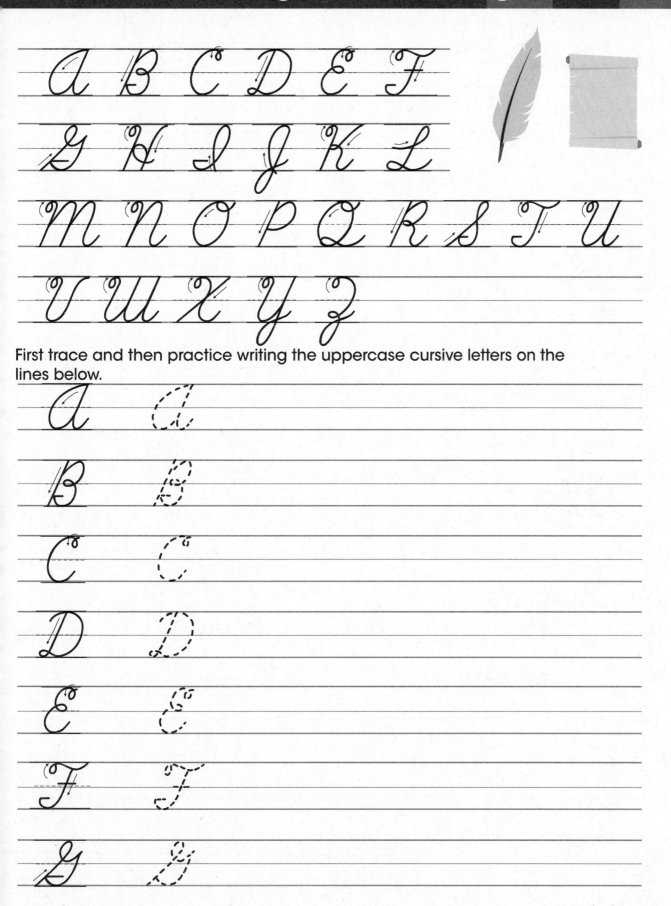

First trace and then practice writing the uppercase cursive letters on the lines below.

Practicing Cursive Writing

First trace and then practice writing the uppercase cursive letters and words on the lines below.

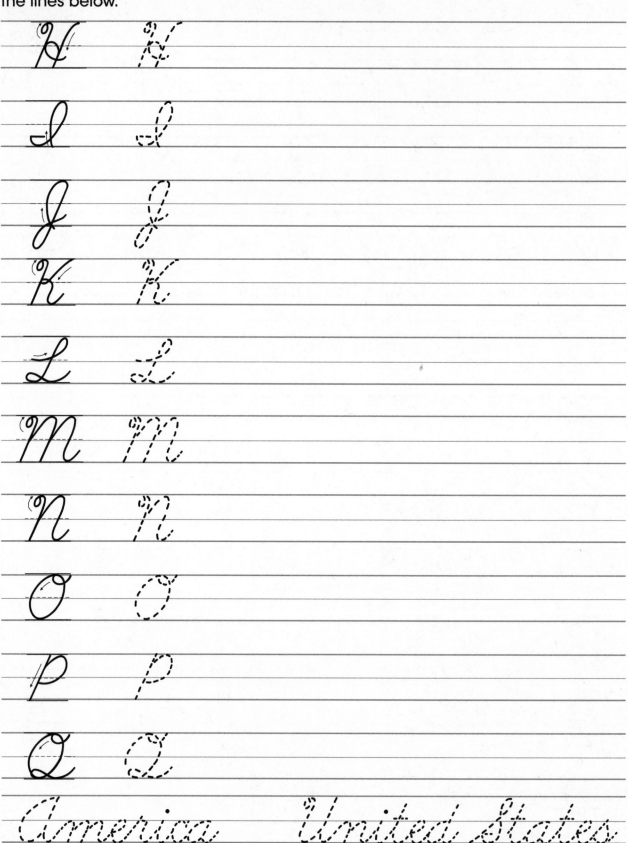

Practicing Cursive Writing

First trace and then practice writing the uppercase cursive letters and words on the lines below.

R   *R*

S   *S*

T   *T*

U   *U*

V   *V*

W   *W*

X   *X*

Y   *Y*

Z   *Z*

California   *New York*

Mississippi   *Oregon*

Print and Cursive

Draw a line to match the print letters to the cursive letters. Then trace the cursive letters.

Print	Cursive
A	*D*
B	*C*
C	*a*
D	*B*
E	*K*
F	*F*
G	*G*
H	*m*
I	*L*
J	*K*
K	*J*
L	*C*
M	

Print	Cursive
N	*P*
O	*Q*
P	*O*
Q	*n*
R	*T*
S	*S*
T	*U*
U	*V*
V	*Y*
W	*Z*
X	*W*
Y	*R*
Z	

Practicing Cursive Writing

Write a Couplet

A couplet is a two-line poem that rhymes.

Trace the couplet poem.

Whiskers

My cat loves to chase a mouse,

especially one that is in my house.

Now write your own couplet poem in cursive on the lines below. Don't forget to give your poem a title.

ABC Order

Putting words into ABC order means they are in the order of the alphabet. If there are multiple words with the same first letter, you need to look at the second letter and sometimes the third letter to put the words in the correct alphabetical order.

Example: diamond   dog   doughnut

Diamond is the first word in ABC order because i comes before o in the alphabet. The remaining two words both have an o after the first letter. Dog is the next word in ABC order because g comes before u in the alphabet. The last word in ABC order is doughnut.

Put all the words in ABC order. Then rewrite them all in order on the lines below.

pole   shell   tusks

sea star   table   apple

pond   apron   turtle

shark   astronaut   porcupine

Titles

Capital Letters for Titles

Movie titles, book titles, and titles of plays or poems are written using a capital letter for almost every word in the title. Only the small words, such as the, to, in, if, and, or, and on are not capitalized, unless one of those words comes at the beginning or end of the title.

Example: Humpty Dumpty

Aladdin and the Magic Lamp

Look at the three movie posters below. Write the title next to each movie poster using correct capitalization.

Coming Soon:

_____

_____

_____

_____

_____

_____

_____

_____

_____

Write your own book title on the lines below. Be sure to capitalize it properly.

_____

_____

Homophones

Homophones **are words that have the** same pronunciation but different spellings **and** different meanings.

Example: sun **and** son

Look at the pictures below and circle the correct homophone word.

see   sea

ate   eight

bear   bare

flour   flower

be   bee

deer   dear

Each sentence below has a word in it that is the wrong homophone. Circle the incorrect homophone and write the correct one on the line after the sentence.

I bought a new (pear) of shoes today! _pair_____

Eye am going skating at the rink tonight. _____

Let's right a letter to a friend. _____

I can't weight for my birthday party next week. _____

Did you sea that shooting star in the sky? _____

I'm going to pick some flours for my mom. _____

Grammar

Homographs

Homographs **are words that have the** same spelling, but different pronunciations **and** different meanings.

Example: bass **and** bass

Look at the two pictures in each box below. Write the correct homograph to complete the two sentences in each box.

I like the pretty _____ in your hair.

A _____ can be a sign of respect.

The _____ is blowing very hard!

My brother will _____ up the toy.

A _____ landed on my windowsill!

Jason _____ into the cold water.

85

Homonyms

Homonyms **are words that have the** same pronunciation **and** the same spelling **but** have different meanings.

Example:  right **and** right

Look at the two pictures in each box below. Write the correct homograph to complete the two sentences in each box.

I wrote a _____ to my best friend.

"I" is a word and a _____ of the alphabet.

A _____ tree can grow very tall.

I have ten cents in my _____.

My dad will _____ our car.

I love to play at the _____.

Grammar

Concrete Nouns Versus Abstract Nouns

Concrete nouns represent people, places, things, or objects that can be seen, heard, touched, tasted, or smelled.

Abstract nouns represent ideas, concepts, or feelings. An idea, concept, or feeling cannot be seen, heard, touched, tasted, or smelled.

Example: Eagle

Eagle is a concrete noun. You can see the eagle.

Freedom

Freedom is an abstract noun. You cannot see freedom, but you can picture something in your mind that represents freedom.

Read each sentence below. Write the sentence's concrete noun in the first column and the abstract noun in the second column.

Sentences	Concrete Nouns	Abstract Nouns
1. The older man enjoyed talking about his childhood.	man	childhood
2. My mom shows her love by giving me a hug.		
3. The lion was experiencing loneliness at the zoo.		
4. The bird rested in peace on the branch.		
5. Tisha found happiness in doing things for others.		
6. The knight was known for his bravery.		
7. Danny thinks getting an education is important.		

Grammar

Comparative Adverbs

Comparative adverbs **are used when** comparing two **of something.**

A comparative adverb **may be a:**

- single **word**
- one-syllable adverb with -er suffix
- phrase

Example: A sundae tastes better than a popsicle. A cheetah is faster than a lion. Dominic paints less carefully than Randall.

worse	more cheaply	longer	as slowly as
less	more seriously	later	as quickly as

Read each sentence below. Use the comparative adverbs in the table above to complete the sentences.

1. The box is _____ than it is tall.

2. Did William finish the race _____ his brother?

3. Getting sick is _____ than getting a shot.

4. The movie starts _____ than the game.

5. Candice took the dance contest _____ than Joseph.

6. The soup did not boil _____ the stew.

7. The shirt fabric was made _____ than the coat fabric.

8. The remote control car costs _____ than the bicycle.

Grammar

Superlative Adjectives

Superlative adjectives **are used when comparing three or more nouns.** Superlative adjectives **are also used when comparing one thing to a group.**

Example: Jupiter is the biggest planet in the solar system.

That was the best movie ever made!

fastest	most happy	least important	worst
deepest	most famous	least sweet	best

Read each sentence below. Use the superlative adjectives in the table above to complete the sentences.

1. The furry dog was the _____ when we came into the room.

2. What is the _____ ocean in the world?

3. I think chocolate is the _____ flavor of ice cream!

4. I think the _____ chore is having to take out smelly garbage!

5. What pitcher has thrown the _____ pitch ever?

6. This pie is the _____ of all the pies we have tasted.

7. The _____ movie cowboy was Roy Rogers.

8. The _____ ingredient in the recipe is the optional cheese topping.

89

Word Relationships

Literal Versus Nonliteral Meanings

Literal meaning means that every word in a sentence conveys exactly what is being said.

Non-literal meaning means that some of the words or a phrase in a sentence conveys something different than what is being said.

Idioms are phrases that convey non-literal meanings.

Example: Cassandra is about to perform her magic act. Mom whispers, "Break a leg," to Cassandra before she goes on stage.

Do you think Cassandra's mom really wants her to break her leg? Of course she doesn't! This is an idiom that means "good luck." You probably have heard idioms before but may have never known that this is what these non-literal phrases are called.

Read the sentences in the left column and underline the idiom (non-literal meaning) in each sentence. In the right column, write what you think the literal meaning is that is being conveyed by the idiom.

Sentences with Idioms	Literal Meaning of Idioms
1. I have <u>butterflies in my stomach</u> because I know the Tilt-a-Whirl will have lots of twists and turns!	This person is nervous about going on a scary ride.
2. Cleaning my room will be a piece of cake because I keep it neat all of the time.	
3. Mr. Andersen looks at the time and says, "It is five o'clock. I think I will call it a day."	
4. "Hang in there!" Brandy shouts to Marcus as he continues to run in the marathon.	
5. Sara, the babysitter, says, "I think Trevor looks a bit under the weather," to Trevor's mother.	

Word Relationships

Word Meaning Nuances

Nuance **means a** slightly different meaning about the same topic or idea. **Words can be grouped based on a topic or idea from the** least to the greatest **intensity based on each word's meaning.**

Example: When you think about describing someone "trying to get someone else's attention," the word meaning nuances from least to greatest could be:

Least	Greater	Still Greater	Greatest
whisper	call	holler	scream

Order each word set below from least to greatest intensity for each topic below.

Topic: move from one place to another
Word Set: run, stroll, walk, jog

Least	Greater	Still Greater	Greatest

Topic: reaction to a birthday party
Word Set: exciting, pleasant, nice, amazing

Least	Greater	Still Greater	Greatest

Topic: how someone might feel at the end of a long day at school
Word Set: exhausted, fatigued, tired, worn-out

Least	Greater	Still Greater	Greatest

Topic: motion of an object moving from one person to another
Word Set: hurl, toss, throw, fling

Least	Greater	Still Greater	Greatest

Writing Sentences

Simple and Compound Sentences

A simple sentence is a sentence with only one clause. A clause is part of a sentence that has a subject (noun or pronoun) and a predicate (verb or verb phrase) in it.

A compound sentence is a sentence with two or more independent clauses.

An independent clause is a clause that has a subject and predicate and forms a complete thought. The two independent clauses are often joined together by a comma and a conjunction (e.g., but, so, for, and). If the conjunction because is used in a compound sentence, there will not be a comma placed before it.

Example: Simple: I saw a pretty bird in the pine tree.

Compound: I saw a pretty bird in the pine tree, but it was not as beautiful as the bird I saw in the tree yesterday.

Read the sentences in the left column. Write simple or compound in the middle column and your reasoning in the right column.

Sentences	Sentence Type	Explain Why
1. Everyone loves to watch Willy play ball, for he can throw a strong pitch.		
2. Jamie ran out of money because he bought too much candy at the store.		
3. The last time I went to the mall I enjoyed playing a lot of video games.		
4. Everyone was busy, so I rode my bike to the park and played alone.		
5. For our celebration dinner, we ate tamales, tostadas, beans, rice, and corn pudding.		

Writing Sentences

Complex Sentences

A complex sentence is a sentence with an independent clause that is joined by a dependent clause.

A dependent clause is a group of words that contains a subject and predicate but cannot stand alone as a complete sentence and does not express a complete thought. Because it is not a complete thought, it depends on an independent clause to form a complete sentence.

An independent clause is a group of words that contains a subject and predicate and expresses a complete thought as a complete sentence.

A complex sentence's dependent clause and independent clause are connected using a subordinating conjunction.

Most Common Subordinating Conjunctions

Timing	Comparison	Condition	Cause/Effect
after/before	although	as long as	as if
once	as	as though	because
since	even though	except	in order to
till/until	like	if	now that
when	rather than	in order for	so
while	though	provided that	whether
whenever	whereas	unless	why

Sometimes the subordinating conjunction will appear at the beginning of a complex sentence.

Example: subordinating conjunction   Sometimes a comma separates the clauses.

(When) the French fries are crispy, take them out of the oven carefully.
      dependent clause   independent clause

This clause could stand alone as a sentence.

Sometimes the subordinating conjunction will appear closer to the middle of a complex sentence.

Example: subordinating conjunction

You will not reach the mountaintop (if) you do not get some rest soon.
      independent clause   dependent clause

This clause could stand alone as a sentence.   Sometimes a comma is not used to separate the clauses.

93

Writing Complex Sentences

For each sentence below:

- **circle the** independent clause in red
- **circle the** dependent clause in blue
- **put a box around the** subordinating conjunction in purple

Even though my friend invited me to the game,
I do not want to go.

I held on to the swing because I felt dizzy.

She giggled loudly as the limber monkey
did a somersault.

The dog jumped up high, so I gave him a tasty treat.

When you are wide awake in the morning,
do a crossword puzzle.

Writing Sentences

Using Commas in Locations and Addresses

A location in a sentence may include a place name, town or city name, state name, and/or country name.

An address in a sentence may include a street address, town or city name, state name, and/or country name.

There needs to be a comma included in between each place in the sentence.

Example: Location: I went to an amusement park in Orlando, Florida, when I was ten years old.

Address: I live at 305 Forest Court, Severna Park, Maryland.

Read the sentences below and add the missing commas.

> We went camping as a family last month in Cincinnati Ohio.
>
> My uncle Manny lives at 1234 Maple Drive Lunenburg Vermont.
>
> Rocking Ranch in Tucson Arizona is a fun place to ride a horse.

Addressing an Envelope

When writing the recipient's address and your return address on an envelope, there only needs to be a comma between the town or city and state.

1. Write the person's full name on the first line.
2. Write the street address on the second line.
3. Write the city, state, and ZIP code on the last line.

Example:

Vicki Jackson
2320 Peachtree Drive
Indianapolis, Indiana 46214

Linda Isaac
777 Paperflower Circle
Lebanon, Indiana 46052

Write your home address neatly in the top-left corner. Who will you be sending your letter to today? Write his or her address neatly in the middle of the envelope. Don't forget to draw a stamp in the top-right corner!

Writing Sentences

Using Commas and Quotation Marks

Quotation marks go around all of the words that people or characters are saying.

Example: "Come over to my house," said Grace.

"Okay," said Ella, "but I can't stay very long."

Commas are used to separate what the person or character is saying from what the narrator is conveying.

Example: "Come over to my house," said Grace.

"Okay," said Ella, "but I can't stay very long."

Read the sentences below. Put quotation marks around what the people or characters are saying. Then add a comma to separate what the narrator is conveying from what the person or character is saying.

I'm hungry said Jacob.

Aaron said Let's go for a swim.

Sammy asked When will we get to the beach?

We are almost there replied Lucas.

Stacey asked What time is it?

Oscar said This is my favorite song!

Sometimes quotation marks go around titles of short stories, songs, poems, and chapters.

Example: My favorite song is "Twinkle, Twinkle, Little Star."

Read the sentences below. Put the quotation marks where they are needed.

I read a lovely poem called My Hungry Heart.

My favorite story is The Princess and the Pea.

I can't get the Chicken Dance song out of my head!

I read chapter eight in The Big Adventure last night.

Have you ever read The Tortoise and the Hare?

If You're Happy and You Know It is my favorite song.

Rules for Writing Dialogue

Remember these basic dialogue rules.

1 **The narrator's text** stays outside the quotation marks, **while the** punctuation stays inside the quotation marks.

Example: "It was an interesting aquarium," Karen explained.

2 **If the narrator's voice comes** before **the dialogue,** a comma appears before the first quotation mark.

Example: Karen explained, "It was an interesting aquarium."

3 **If the dialogue** ends with an exclamation point or a question mark, **the narrator's text** begins with a lowercase letter **and the dialogue punctuation** will stay inside the quotation marks.

Example: "It was an amazing aquarium!" exclaimed Karen.

4 **When a quotation is** separated into two parts **with words like "he asked" or "the magician said,"** the second part begins with a lowercase letter.

Example: "What are some of the things," Mom inquired, "that you saw at the aquarium today?"

"One thing I saw," replied Sarah, "was a leopard shark!"

5 **Anytime there is a** change **in which character is speaking,** a new indented paragraph is needed **with** one empty line space between the two paragraphs.

Example: "Was it an interesting aquarium?" asked Mom.

"It was an amazing aquarium!" exclaimed Karen.

6 **If a character** performs an action after speaking, **keep the character's action in the** same paragraph. **Then move to a new line and start the next paragraph** when another character begins speaking or if the narrator starts explaining. **This helps readers know who is speaking and who is performing the action.**

Example: "Karen, I am going to have to go to this aquarium someday soon," said Mom. She reached for the brochure that Karen had brought home.

"Oh yes!" squealed Karen. Her eyes focused on the brochure's cover. She mentioned excitedly, "The best part of the aquarium is the jellyfish exhibit!"

Although she had a full calendar of events for the month, Karen's mom decided it would be great family fun to go to the aquarium, so she arranged a time for them to go next Saturday.

Writing Sentences

Time to Write Dialogue

The sentences in the box are missing quotation marks and indented paragraphs to separate the character's dialogue from the narrator's voice.

Randy's brother, Micah, picked him up from school on Friday. They then drove to their sister's school to pick her up. Micah greeted her as she hopped into the car, Hi, Andrea! Hi, Micah, she responded, and hi to you, too, Randy. Mom told me before I left that it might rain this weekend, Micah informed his siblings. Does that mean we won't be going camping? mumbled Andrea. I hope we still get to go! exclaimed Randy. Calm down, Randy, reassured Micah, we are still going to go, even if the weather is bad. We are staying in a cabin this time, not in a tent, remember?

Here is the text rewritten using the dialogue rules.

Randy's brother, Micah, picked him up from school on Friday. They then drove to their sister's school to pick her up. Micah greeted her as she hopped into the car, "Hi, Andrea!"

"Hi, Micah," she responded, "and hi to you, too, Randy."

"Mom told me before I left that it might rain this weekend," Micah informed his siblings.

"Does that mean we won't be going camping?" mumbled Andrea.

"I hope we still get to go!" exclaimed Randy.

"Calm down, Randy," reassured Micah, "we are still going to go, even if the weather is bad. We are staying in a cabin this time, not in a tent, remember?"

Writing Sentences

Now it is your turn. Read the sentences in the blue box below. Rewrite the sentences using the dialogue rules. Hint: There will be four paragraphs.

Mindy's mother came into the kitchen and tied the apron strings around her daughter's waist. Mindy, I think you're old enough to make our dinner rolls now. Really, Momma? squealed Mindy. I will be right here to help you, encouraged her mother, if you get stuck and are not sure what to do. Thank you, Momma! What is the first thing I need to do? inquired Mindy.

The Writing Process

Good writers follow a sequence of steps to create a variety of writing types.

Brainstorm

Think about what you want to write about and what you want to say. Use a graphic organizer to plan out your ideas.

Draft

Look at your graphic organizer and write out the first draft of your story.

Revise

Read your draft and make changes to improve your writing.

Edit

Proofread your revised draft and correct any grammar, punctuation, or capitalization errors.

Publish

Rewrite your draft as a final copy using a pencil and paper, a computer, or a tablet.

The Writing Process

Edit and Revise

Revising **is** reading your own or someone else's writing **and seeing where it can be** improved for ideas, descriptions, or explanations.
Editing **is** looking for grammar and punctuation errors **and** marking them **to be corrected.**

Revise

Add sentences or words.

Remove unneeded sentences or words.

Move sentences around to make the text make more sense.

Change boring words to exciting words so readers are more engaged.

Edit

Be sure to capitalize the beginning of sentences, names, titles, and proper nouns.

Be sure to use simple, compound, and complex sentences.

Be sure to use periods, question marks, exclamation points, commas, and quotation marks correctly.

Be sure to check the spelling of all words to make certain they are correct.

Editing Marks

When you reread your writing, you will need a colored pencil or pen. Use your editor's checklist to look for mistakes. When you notice something that needs to be changed, mark it with the appropriate proofreading mark below.

PROOFREADING MARKS

Capital Letter	Lowercase Letter	Add Comma	Add Quotation Marks	Delete
Add Period	Add Question Mark	Add Exclamation Point	sp. Spelling Error	New Paragraph
Make Space	Close Up Space	Reverse Letters/Words	Insert Word	Insert a Letter

A Sample Revision

Here is an example of the beginning of an informational text draft that has been revised and edited using proofreading marks. While a blue pen is used here to create the marks, you can use any color that shows up well.

Title **Elephants Around the World**

Their are three species of
sp. There
elephants. Two of them live in

africa, and one lives in asia. How

can you Tell the diference

between an asian and african

elephant? Look at the ears!

An asian elephants ears

aremuch smaller than an african
#
elephants ears ears.

Revising and Editing Writing

Read the passage. Use the checklist and proofreading marks to help Liberty revise and edit her draft. Then draw a picture to match the passage below.

Why Liberty Loves Independence Day

My name is liberty becauz my parents met at the statue of liberty in new york city New York. july 4th is independence day, and it is my favorite holiday! My whole family had fun together all day and night this year. We went to the park wear we herd a band play patriotic songs, including america the beautiful. There were lots of families there and lots of activities, like a balloon toss. My sister and I were in a three-legged race, but we fell down and didn't win. Then we had a piknik dinner and ice cream for dessert. When it got dark, there was a fireworks show. That was the best part. There was even a special display of the Liberty Statue in bright lights, so my sister said I was in the show.

Brainstorming for Narrative Writing

Narrative writing is writing a story with a beginning, middle, and end.

Fill in the graphic organizer to help you brainstorm ideas to write a short story. Think of a time you went to an exciting place. What happened first, next, then, and last? Write a few words or phrases in each box to remind yourself about the main points of each section to include in your story.

Title _____

First

_____
_____
_____
_____

Next

_____
_____
_____
_____

Then

_____
_____
_____
_____

Last

_____
_____
_____

The Writing Process

Time to Write a Narrative Story

This will be your first draft. Look at your graphic organizer and write your story on the lines below and on the next pages. Be sure to use a variety of sentence types (simple, compound, and complex).

Title_____

Opening
_____
_____
_____
_____
_____

First
_____
_____
_____
_____
_____
_____
_____
_____
_____
_____
_____
_____
_____
_____

Next
_____
_____
_____
_____
_____
_____
_____

(cont.)

_____
_____
_____
_____

Then
_____
_____
_____
_____
_____
_____
_____
_____
_____
_____

Last
_____
_____
_____
_____
_____
_____
_____
_____
_____
_____

Time to Revise and Edit

Using the proofreading marks below, re-read your draft and make any necessary revisions and edits using a colored pencil or pen.

PROOFREADING MARKS

☰ Capital Letter	/ Lowercase Letter	⌃, Add Comma
⊙ Add Period	? Add Question Mark	! Add Exclamation Point
# Make Space	⌒ Close Up Space	∿ Reverse Letters/Words
⌃ of Insert Word	∨ ∨ Add Quotation Marks	Delete
/ Insert a Letter	sp. Spelling Error	¶ New Paragraph

Publishing

Rewrite your draft as a final copy using a pencil or pen, or by typing on a computer or tablet. Share your narrative story with your family and friends!

Expository Writing

Brainstorming for Expository Writing

Expository writing **is writing about** a person, place, thing, or event that you know about or have researched in detail **and will be** explaining to the reader.

Think about an animal, person, or historical event you know a lot about or have researched. Now write your topic in the red oval. What will your three subtopics be? Write each one in a subtopic box. Then write a few words or phrases in each fact box to organize your thoughts. Lastly, write a few concluding thoughts in the rectangular conclusion box.

Introduction

Topic

Fact 2

Supporting Detail

Subtopic 1

Fact 1

Supporting Detail

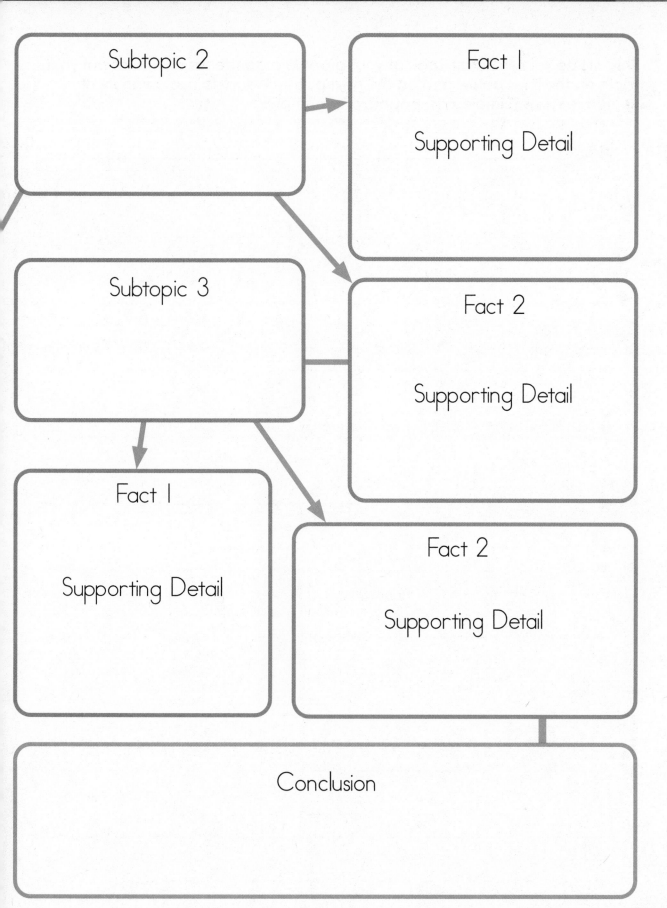

Subtopic 2

Fact 1

Supporting Detail

Subtopic 3

Fact 2

Supporting Detail

Fact 1

Supporting Detail

Fact 2

Supporting Detail

Conclusion

Expository Writing

Time to Write an Expository Text

This will be your first draft. Look at your graphic organizer and write about your topic on the lines below and on the next page. Be sure to use a variety of sentence types (simple, compound, and complex).

Title_____

_____

_____

_____

_____

_____

_____

_____

_____

_____

_____

_____

_____

_____

_____

_____

_____

_____

_____

_____

_____

_____

_____

_____

_____

_____
_____
_____
_____
_____
_____
_____
_____
_____
_____
_____
_____
_____
_____
_____
_____

Time to Revise and Edit

Using the proofreading marks below, re-read your draft and make any necessary revisions and edits with a colored pencil or pen.

PROOFREADING MARKS

Capital Letter	Lowercase Letter	Add Comma	Add Quotation Marks	Delete
Add Period	Add Question Mark	Add Exclamation Point	sp. Spelling Error	New Paragraph
Make Space	Close Up Space	Reverse Letters/Words	Insert Word	Insert a Letter

Publishing

Rewrite your draft as a final copy using a pencil or pen, or by typing on a computer or tablet. Share your expository writing with your family and friends!

Brainstorming for Opinion Writing

Opinion writing **is writing about** something you believe and can provide reasons and details to support your thinking. **An opinion can be about something** you like **or something** you do not like.

Example: I love to eat pickles, but my brother does not. I could write an opinion about why pickles are super tasty. My brother would write an opinion about why pickles are not tasty.

What is your opinion about something you like or do not like? It can be about anything, such as a game, a sport, a television show, a movie, a book, or food. Write your opinion statement in the first box. Then write a few words or phrases in each reason box to organize your thoughts. Be sure to add linking phrases that will connect each of your reasons. Lastly, write your concluding thoughts.

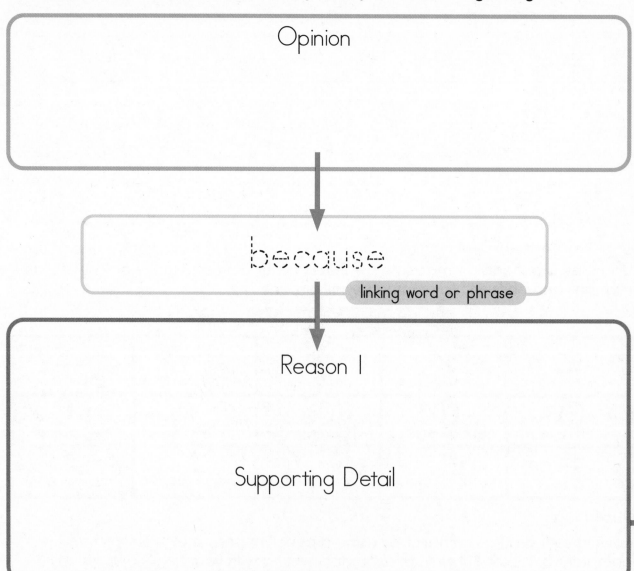

Opinion

because

linking word or phrase

Reason I

Supporting Detail

Another important point is

linking word or phrase

Reason 2

Supporting Detail

I also think that

linking word or phrase

Reason 3

Supporting Detail

Conclusion

Opinion Writing

Time to Write an Opinion Text

This will be the first draft. Look at your graphic organizer and write your opinion, reasons, and supporting details on the lines below and on the next pages. Be sure to use a variety of sentence types (simple, compound, and complex).

Title_____

Opinion Writing

_____
_____
_____
_____
_____
_____
_____
_____
_____
_____
_____
_____
_____
_____
_____
_____
_____
_____
_____
_____

Time to Revise and Edit

Using the proofreading marks below, re-read your draft and make any necessary revisions and edits with a colored pencil or pen.

PROOFREADING MARKS

Capital Letter	Lowercase Letter	Add Comma	Add Quotation Marks	Delete
Add Period	Add Question Mark	Add Exclamation Point	sp. Spelling Error	New Paragraph
Make Space	Close Up Space	Reverse Letters/Words	Insert Word	Insert a Letter

Publishing

Rewrite your draft as a final copy using a pencil or pen, or by typing on a computer or tablet. Share your opinion writing with your family and friends!

Poetry Writing

Poetry

There are many different kinds of poetry. Three fun structures are acrostic poems, shape poems, and haikus.

Acrostic Poems

An acrostic poem has a word vertically down the left side. The word is the subject of the poem. Each letter in the word becomes the first letter of a line in the poem.

Example:

Love is a feeling to celebrate, not

Only on

Valentine's Day each year.

Everyone deserves to feel loved!

Shape Poems

A shape poem is a poem that takes the shape of what the poem is about. It is a poem and an illustration at the same time!

Example:

Pie

cut

into 8

tasty slices

makes friends

smile and laugh

and goes great with

a nice cold glass of milk

Haiku

A haiku is a Japanese poem. It has three lines that follow a pattern of syllables.

Line 1: 5 syllables   **Line 2: 7 syllables**   **Line 3: 5 syllables**

Example:

Hot butter in pan,

Sliced bread, milk, egg, cinnamon,

Butter, syrup, YUM!

Writing Poetry

Write your own poems below.

My Acrostic Poem

My Shape Poem

My Haiku

_____

_____ (5 syllables)

_____

_____ (7 syllables)

_____

_____ (5 syllables)

Procedural Writing

Procedural writing **is writing** directions for doing something.

In procedural writing, it is important to be very descriptive. **You must also be sure to** write the steps in the correct order.

Read the procedural writing below and visualize or try to follow the directions.

Wrapping a Gift

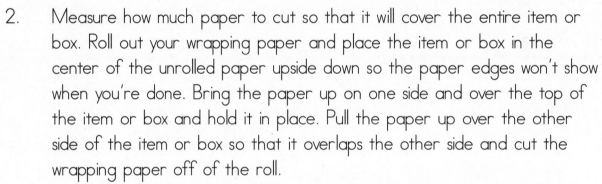

Materials Needed:

Present, wrapping paper, scissors, tape

1. Pack any breakable materials carefully. Make sure that anything fragile is protected and won't move around or become damaged when you are wrapping the present.

2. Measure how much paper to cut so that it will cover the entire item or box. Roll out your wrapping paper and place the item or box in the center of the unrolled paper upside down so the paper edges won't show when you're done. Bring the paper up on one side and over the top of the item or box and hold it in place. Pull the paper up over the other side of the item or box so that it overlaps the other side and cut the wrapping paper off of the roll.

3. Secure the paper to the item or box with tape. Tape one edge of the paper to the bottom side of the item or box. Make a clean seam on the other side of the paper by folding over the last half inch of the paper and using your fingers to create a tight crease. Now bring this side up so it just overlaps the already taped-down edge and tape the creased edge down.

4. Fold the paper on each end of the present. Starting on one side, fold down the top flap and then the bottom flap onto the side of the item or box to create two little wings on that side. Flatten one of the wings against the item or box, then fold the other wing of paper up against the box. Tape the folded wings into place.

5. Stand the item or box up and fold the paper on the other end. Repeat step 4 on the opposite end.

6. If desired, add ribbon and a decorative bow to your gift.

Procedural Writing

Writing How-To Instructions

Choose a how-to topic that you know well. It could be how to follow a recipe, how to lace your shoes, how to do a card trick, or how to do a dance move. Write the detailed steps on the lines below and on the next page.

How-To Topic Title
_____
_____

Materials Needed:
_____
_____
_____
_____

Steps
_____
_____
_____
_____
_____
_____
_____
_____
_____
_____
_____
_____
_____
_____
_____

(cont.)

_____

_____

_____

_____

_____

_____

_____

_____

_____

_____

_____

_____

_____

_____

_____

_____

_____

_____

Draw an illustration to help a reader follow your how-to directions.

Descriptive Writing

Descriptive Writing

Descriptive writing **paints a** picture in your mind of how something looks, feels, smells, sounds, and sometimes tastes.

Read the passage below and see if you get a picture in your mind of what is about to be eaten based on the descriptive details. Be sure to STOP and write what you are thinking *after* you read a sentence or paragraph *before* you start reading the next sentence or paragraph.

Ooey, Gooey Happiness!
By Jaella Wells

My eyes are excited about what I see in front of me! It is a circular shape and made of yummy layers of deliciousness!

STOP! What are some foods the narrator may be about to eat based on the opening description?

_____

_____

I see a thick, wavy shape around the edge that looks like some kind of dough.

STOP! What foods may the narrator still be about to eat based on the second description?

_____

_____

On top of the dough, it looks like there are miniature brown balls floating by orange canoes on a big red lake.

STOP! What food do you think the narrator is eating now based on the additional description?

_____

_____

I pull a triangle away from the circle and bring it to my mouth. My first bite explodes with the yummy flavors of peppery meat, sharp cheesiness, and fresh tomatoey spices. It fills my tummy with ooey, gooey happiness!

STOP! What descriptions in the last paragraph helped you confirm your food prediction is correct?

_____

_____

Descriptive Writing

Brainstorming Your Descriptive Writing

Now that you have read the descriptive writing "Ooey, Gooey Happiness," did you predict Jaella ate a slice of pizza?

_____ Yes   _____ No

The more descriptive words and phrases you use purposefully in your writing, the better readers can imagine in their minds what you are wanting them to see, feel, smell, and taste.

Now it is time for you to write about something you like to eat. Answer the questions below using words or phrases to help you plan your descriptive writing passage.

> ## What food will you be describing? What will your title be?
> *Remember not to use the name of your food in the title or passage because that will give it away!*
>
> _____
> _____
> _____
> _____
>
> ## What does it look like?
>
> _____
> _____
> _____
> _____
>
> ## What does it feel like?
>
> _____
> _____
> _____
> _____
>
> ## What does it smell like?
>
> _____
> _____
> _____
> _____
>
> ## What does it taste like?
>
> _____
> _____
> _____
> _____

Write Your Own Descriptive Writing

Using your brainstorming notes to help you, write your descriptive passage on the lines below. After you are done writing your passage, share your food description with a family member or friend and see if he or she can guess what food you are describing!

Title_____

_____

_____

_____

_____

_____

_____

_____

_____

_____

_____

_____

_____

_____

_____

_____

_____

_____

_____

_____

_____

_____

_____

_____

_____

_____

Reading a Fable

A fable is a short story with a moral or lesson. Fables often include a narrator's voice, one or two main characters, and possibly other characters. All of the characters are usually animals. A fable may have one setting for the entire story or may have several settings.

When characters talk like humans in fables, what they say is called dialogue and is inside quotation marks. A character's dialogue usually starts on a separate line and is indented.

On the next few pages, you will read a famous fable called "The Tortoise and the Hare." To help you notice who is talking and when, the narrator's voice; the two main characters, Hare and Tortoise; and the other character, Fox, have their text identified in different colors.

Narrator	Hare	Tortoise	Fox
purple text	blue text	brown text	red text

The Tortoise and the Hare

One afternoon, Hare is making fun of Tortoise. "You are sooooo sloooow!" Hare chuckles. He then asks, "Do you ever get anywhere?"

Tortoise turns his head slightly and eyes Hare. He says in a calm voice, "I may be slow, but I get where I am going sooner than you think."

Both Hare and Tortoise look up at a poster they notice on a nearby fence at the same time. It reads:

County Race
Saturday at Noon
Everyone Is Welcome!

"Let's run in the race and see who wins between the two of us," suggests Tortoise.

"I think that is a great idea, Tortoise, and I already

know who will win," Hare responds with a mocking laugh.

When they arrive at the county fairgrounds on Saturday, there are lots of animals ready to run in the race. Everyone makes their way toward the starting line, including Hare and Tortoise. They spread out under a banner that reads "START."

Fox, the official racing judge, shouts through a megaphone, "Welcome creatures great and small! Are you ready to race?" A roar is heard throughout the crowd. "Alright then...On your mark, get set, goooo!"

Some creatures begin running quickly, while others run slowly. Hare is running with the speedy group, while Tortoise is taking his time and enjoying running with some snails.

When Hare arrives at the top of a grassy hill, he looks back and comments amusingly, "I can't see Tortoise anywhere!" He decides he has plenty of time to take a nap. "I will take a snooze in this soft, fluffy grass."

Tortoise continues running at a slow pace, and over time, passes right by snoring Hare! Hare keeps sleeping peacefully for another fifteen minutes. When he finally wakes up, he sees there are no runners running by him. "What's happened?" Hare shouts.

He looks down the path on the other side of the grassy hill and sees Tortoise nearing the finish line banner. "Oh nooo!" screeches Hare as he dashes down the path as swiftly as his paws can carry him. Just as Hare is about to overtake him, Tortoise crosses the finish line!

During the awards ceremony, Fox announces, "Ladies and gentlemen, Hare and Tortoise had a race within a race today to see who runs the fastest, and Tortoise won by a hair!" Everyone cheers, and Tortoise is then awarded a special trophy by Fox.

"Thank you, Fox, for my special award," Tortoise says from the heart, "and thank you, Hare, for running a race with me. Now let's go and nibble on some tasty lettuce together."

What do you think is the moral, or lesson, of the fable?

Put a check in one of the two boxes and explain why you chose that moral or lesson using phrases from the fable.

☐ Slow and steady wins the race.

☐ Small friends may prove to be great friends.

_____
_____
_____
_____
_____
_____
_____
_____
_____

Writing a Fable

Brainstorming to Write a Fable

Sometimes the hardest part about writing a fable is coming up with the moral or lesson you want readers to learn. It helps when you try out your moral or lesson ideas on family members or friends first. On your own or with a friend, decide what the moral or lesson of your story is going to be. Write it on the lines below.

The moral or lesson of my fable will be:

_____

_____

_____

_____

Now that you know your fable's moral or lesson, you need to decide who your characters are and what your fable's problem and solution will be.

Example: Problem: The tortoise is slow and unlikely to win the race.

Solution: He never gives up, and he eventually wins the race because he never stops trying.

Answer the questions on the lines below to complete your fable outline.

Who are the main characters of your fable?

_____

_____

_____

_____

_____

My fable's problem is:

_____

_____

_____

My fable's solution will be:

_____

_____

_____

_____

Writing a Fable

Answer the questions on the lines below to complete your fable outline.

Will your fable have one or more settings? List them here:

_____

_____

_____

How will your narrator's voice introduce your main character or characters?

_____

_____

_____

How will the narrator describe the first (or only) setting?

_____

_____

_____

What will be some of the dialogue that will support how the problem arises?

_____

_____

_____

_____

What are some of the details the narrator will explain so readers know the fable's problem has been resolved?

_____

_____

_____

_____

Writing a Fable

Time to Write a Fable

This will be the first draft. Using your brainstorming notes, write your fable on the lines provided on the next few pages. Be sure to use a variety of sentence types (simple, compound, and complex).

Title _____

_____

_____

_____

_____

_____

_____

_____

_____

_____

_____

_____

_____

_____

_____

_____

_____

_____

_____

_____

_____

_____

_____

_____

_____

_____

_____

_____

_____

_____

_____

_____

_____

Writing a Fable

Reminder: Don't forget that each time you use dialogue for a character, you will most likely need to start writing the text on a new line, with one empty line space in between the last paragraph and the new paragraph! Also, do not forget to indent each new paragraph, even when the paragraph is only dialogue and the narrator's voice.

(cont.)

(cont.)

(cont.)

_____

_____

_____

_____

_____

_____

_____

_____

_____

The moral of the story is:

_____

_____

_____

Time to Revise and Edit

Using the proofreading marks below, re-read your draft and make any necessary revisions and edits with a colored pencil or pen.

PROOFREADING MARKS

≡ Capital Letter	/ Lowercase Letter	˄ Add Comma	" " Add Quotation Marks	Delete
⊙ Add Period	⟨?⟩ Add Question Mark	⟨!⟩ Add Exclamation Point	sp. Spelling Error	¶ New Paragraph
# Make Space	⌒ Close Up Space	Reverse Letters/Words	˄ Insert Word	Insert a Letter

Publishing

Rewrite your draft as a final copy using a pencil or pen, or by typing on a computer or tablet. Share your fable with your family and friends!

Journal Writing

Journal Writing

Sometimes writing your feelings down in a journal can be a great way to express yourself.

Write about how you're feeling today on the lines below and on the next page.

_____
_____
_____
_____
_____
_____
_____
_____
_____
_____
_____
_____
_____
_____
_____
_____
_____
_____
_____
_____
_____
_____
_____
_____
_____
_____
_____
_____

(cont.)

_____
_____
_____
_____
_____
_____
_____
_____
_____
_____
_____
_____
_____
_____
_____
_____
_____
_____
_____
_____
_____

Draw a picture of something you wrote about during your journal writing time.

CERTIFICATE
of Achievement

....

has succesfully completed

3rd Grade Writing

Date:

Signed:

1²3 Math

Table of Contents

Third Grade Math Readiness

Third grade is an important year for math. This year is the bridge from foundational skills to more complex math. Children are using the foundational skills they have acquired and building on them to acquire new skills.

There is immense value in talking positively about math. Utilize math skills as often as possible to support your student's or child's grasp of number sense and number operations. Environmental math games, such as adding up license plate numbers, and playing strategic-thinking games, such as chess, are great activities for third grade mathematicians.

Least to Greatest

Put the numbers in order from least to greatest. Write the numbers on the lines below.

Example:

 1,245   1,552   1,876   3,281

2,432 1,567 3,253 7,119	_____, _____, _____, _____
6,547 1,734 5,087 2,891	_____, _____, _____, _____
2,322 1,845 4,137 7,678	_____, _____, _____, _____
4,688 4,156 3,273 5,449	_____, _____, _____, _____
9,555 5,381 1,291 8,762	_____, _____, _____, _____

Number Hunt

Find the numbers that match the descriptions. Write the numbers on the lines below.

2,625	4,275	1,439
7,443	6,217	5,000

The number between 2,000 and 3,000 is ___2,625___.

The number that has 0 tens and 0 ones is _____.

The number between 1,000 and 1,500 is _____.

The number between 4,000 and 5,000 is _____.

The number that has 7 ones is _____.

The number greater than all the others numbers is _____.

Number Sense

Thousands, Hundreds, Tens, and Ones

Example:

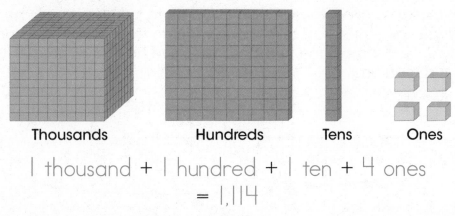

Thousands   Hundreds   Tens   Ones

1 thousand + 1 hundred + 1 ten + 4 ones
= 1,114

Use the models below to count and write how many thousands, hundreds, tens, and ones there are on the lines below.

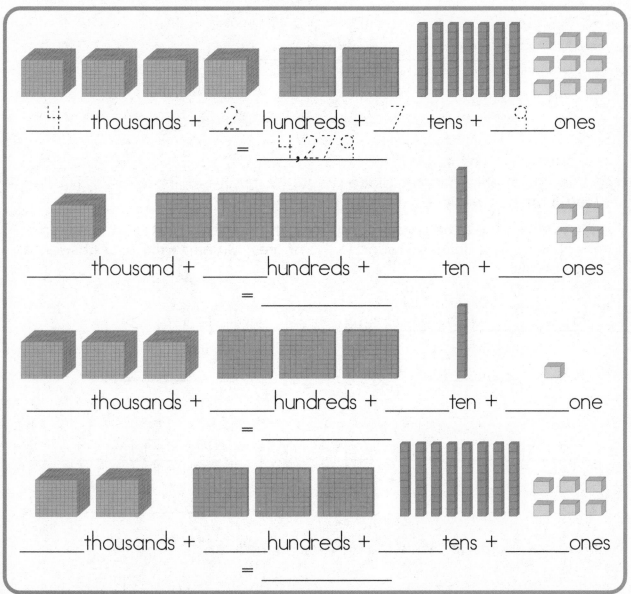

___4___ thousands + ___2___ hundreds + ___7___ tens + ___9___ ones
= ___4,279___

_____ thousand + _____ hundreds + _____ ten + _____ ones
= _____

_____ thousands + _____ hundreds + _____ ten + _____ one
= _____

_____ thousands + _____ hundreds + _____ tens + _____ ones
= _____

Rounding to the Nearest Ten

Sometimes we use rounding to make an estimate to tell about how much a number is. When you round, you take the number to the nearest ten, hundred, or thousand, etc. Take a look at the number line to see how you can use it to help you understand rounding.

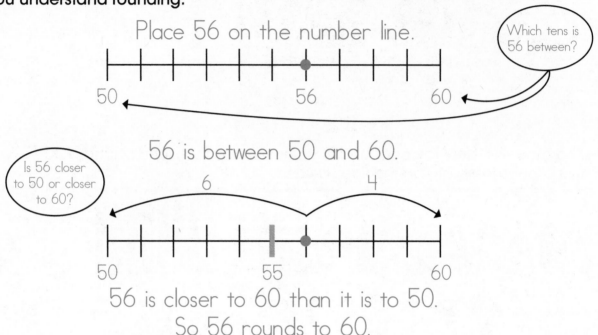

Place 56 on the number line.

Which tens is 56 between?

56 is between 50 and 60.

Is 56 closer to 50 or closer to 60?

56 is closer to 60 than it is to 50.
So 56 rounds to 60.

HINT: If the number in the ones place is equal to or greater than 5, round up to the next ten. If the number is less than 5, round down.

Use the number line to help you round. Read the numbers and mark them on the number lines with a dot. Then round to the nearest ten and write your answers on the lines below.

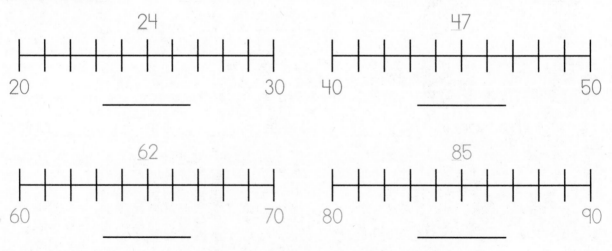

Round to the nearest ten. Write the answers on the lines.

57 _____   34 _____   82 _____   75 _____

Rounding to the Nearest Hundred

You can use what you learned from rounding to the nearest ten to help you round to the nearest hundred. Use the number line to help you know when to round up or round down. Remember, rounding is used to make an estimate.

Place 372 on the number line.

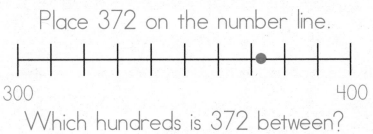

Which hundreds is 372 between?

To round, ask yourself if 372 is closer to 300 or 400. It is closer to 400, so 372 rounds to 400. You can also look at the number in the tens place. If the number is equal to or greater than 50, you will round up. 372 has 70 in the tens place, which is greater than 50, so it needs to be rounded up to 400.

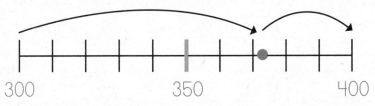

Use the number line to help you round. Read the numbers and mark them on the number lines with a dot. Then round to the nearest hundred and write your answers on the lines below.

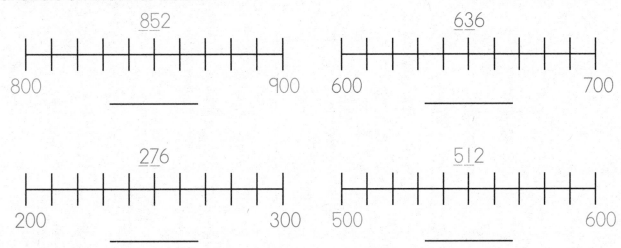

852

800   900

636

600   700

276

200   300

512

500   600

Round to the nearest hundred. Write the answers on the lines below.

467 _____   298 _____   553 _____   725 _____

The baby giraffe weighs 341 pounds. What is its weight rounded to the nearest hundred pounds? _____ pounds

Expanded Notation

You can show numbers in expanded form in two different ways. Numbers can be written in words or written to show their separate place values.

Example: 4,393 = 4000 + 300 + 90 + 3

4,393 = four thousand + three hundred + ninety + three

Write the numbers in expanded form using place value numbers on the lines below.

3,596 = __3000__ + __500__ + __90__ + __6__

2,185 = _____ + _____ + _____ + _____

4,526 = _____ + _____ + _____ + _____

1,732 = _____ + _____ + _____ + _____

4,444 = _____ + _____ + _____ + _____

Write the numbers in expanded form using words on the lines below.

5,276 = __five__ + __two__ + __seven__ + __six__
         thousands   hundreds   tens   ones

3,121 = _____ + _____ + _____ + _____
         thousands   hundreds   tens   ones

2,349 = _____ + _____ + _____ + _____
         thousands   hundreds   tens   ones

1,587 = _____ + _____ + _____ + _____
         thousands   hundreds   tens   ones

1,995 = _____ + _____ + _____ + _____
         thousands   hundreds   tens   ones

Addition and Subtraction

Adding and Subtracting Three-Digit Numbers

Practice adding and subtracting three-digit numbers. Write the answers in the boxes below.

Hundreds	Tens	Ones
3	2	1
+ 4	3	7

Hundreds	Tens	Ones
4	2	6
− 3	1	3

Hundreds	Tens	Ones
7	0	3
+ 1	1	3

Hundreds	Tens	Ones
7	1	4
− 5	1	3

Hundreds	Tens	Ones
2	9	9
− 1	0	7

Hundreds	Tens	Ones
4	6	2
+ 3	1	6

Hundreds	Tens	Ones
6	3	7
− 5	2	2

Hundreds	Tens	Ones
4	3	6
+ 2	6	2

Hundreds	Tens	Ones
5	5	3
− 4	3	2

Answer the number sense questions and write your answers on the lines.

What number is in the tens place of the number 274? _____

What number is in the ones place of the number 680? _____

What number is in the hundreds place of the number 175? _____

How many tens are in the number 369? _____

145

Addition and Subtraction

Adding Three-Digit Numbers by Regrouping

Adding hundreds, tens, and ones sometimes involves regrouping. If the numbers in a column add up to more than 9, you need to regroup to the next higher place value.

Solve the problems by regrouping. Write the answers in the boxes below.

Hundreds	Tens	Ones
	1	
1	2	6
+ 1	4	7
2	7	3

Hundreds	Tens	Ones
2	4	5
+ 5	3	7

Hundreds	Tens	Ones
3	2	4
+ 4	3	7

Hundreds	Tens	Ones
4	6	5
+ 3	1	6

Hundreds	Tens	Ones
7	0	8
+ 2	1	3

Hundreds	Tens	Ones
4	3	6
+ 3	6	5

Hundreds	Tens	Ones
5	3	6
+ 2	1	6

Hundreds	Tens	Ones
2	7	9
+ 6	4	4

Hundreds	Tens	Ones
2	5	6
+ 4	1	6

Solve the word problem and write the equation and the sum in the box.

Olivia is having a big party!
She is buying party hats for everyone.
She buys 178 silver party hats and 352 gold party hats. How many party hats did Olivia buy altogether?

Hundreds	Tens	Ones
+		

Addition and Subtraction

Adding Three-Digit Numbers with Regrouping Using Place Value

You can use place value to help you add multi-digit numbers when you need to regroup.

Example:
$$256 + 538 = 200 + 50 + 6$$
$$\underline{500 + 30 + 8}$$
$$700 + 80 + 14 = 794$$

Solve the equations below by using the place-value strategy and write the answers on the lines.

126 + 147 =

_____ + _____ + _____

_____ + _____ + _____

_____ + _____ + _____ = _____

245 + 537 =

_____ + _____ + _____

_____ + _____ + _____

_____ + _____ + _____ = _____

708 + 213 =

_____ + _____ + _____

_____ + _____ + _____

_____ + _____ + _____ = _____

279 + 610 =

_____ + _____ + _____

_____ + _____ + _____

_____ + _____ + _____ = _____

324 + 437 =

_____ + _____ + _____

_____ + _____ + _____

_____ + _____ + _____ = _____

436 + 355 =

_____ + _____ + _____

_____ + _____ + _____

_____ + _____ + _____ = _____

Solve the word problem by using the place-value strategy and write the equation and the sum on the lines.

Alison is also having a big party! She has 178 red party hats and 312 blue party hats. How many hats does Alison have for her party?

_____ + _____ + _____

_____ + _____ + _____

_____ + _____ + _____ = _____

Subtracting Three-Digit Numbers by Regrouping

Subtracting hundreds, tens, and ones sometimes involves regrouping. If the top number in a column is less than the bottom number, you need to regroup by borrowing from the next higher place value.

Solve the equations by regrouping. Write the differences in the boxes below.

Hundreds	Tens	Ones
	3	16
2	4̶	6̶
− 1	1	8
1	2	8

Hundreds	Tens	Ones
4	2	2
− 3	1	4

Hundreds	Tens	Ones
5	1	3
− 4	3	5

Hundreds	Tens	Ones
7	1	4
− 5	3	7

Hundreds	Tens	Ones
2	9	5
− 1	2	7

Hundreds	Tens	Ones
6	3	1
− 5	2	5

Hundreds	Tens	Ones
8	1	3
− 3	0	5

Hundreds	Tens	Ones
4	2	4
− 3	3	3

Hundreds	Tens	Ones
6	1	3
− 2	7	6

Solve the word problem and write the problem and the answer in the box.

Olivia needs to inflate 594 balloons for her party. She takes a break after inflating 276 balloons. How many balloons does she still need to inflate?

Hundreds	Tens	Ones
−		

Addition and Subtraction

Adding to Check Subtraction

You can use related facts to help you check your
answer to an addition or subtraction equation.

Think *addition*
to check
subtraction.

Example: If $435 - 123 = 312$ then $312 + 123 = 435$

Solve the subtraction equations and then check your answers using addition.
Write the numbers on the lines below.

$555 - 434 = \underline{121}$
$\underline{121} + \underline{434} = \underline{555}$

$580 - 240 = \underline{}$
$\underline{} + \underline{} = \underline{}$

$359 - 327 = \underline{}$
$\underline{} + \underline{} = \underline{}$

$487 - 316 = \underline{}$
$\underline{} + \underline{} = \underline{}$

$398 - 265 = \underline{}$
$\underline{} + \underline{} = \underline{}$

$768 - 542 = \underline{}$
$\underline{} + \underline{} = \underline{}$

$678 - 323 = \underline{}$
$\underline{} + \underline{} = \underline{}$

$589 - 254 = \underline{}$
$\underline{} + \underline{} = \underline{}$

Solve the word problem and write the equation and the answer on the lines below.

Anthony and Rebecca collected 423 shells while walking on
the beach. They gave Nicole 123 of them to start a collection
of her own. How many seashells do Anthony and Rebecca
still have in their collection?

$\underline{} - \underline{} = \underline{}$
$\underline{} + \underline{} = \underline{}$

149

Addition and Subtraction

Addition and Subtraction Word Problems

Read each word problem carefully and look for clues to help you know if you should add or subtract. Numbers and words can be clues!

Circle the clues and use them to decide which operation and symbol you will use in your equation. Solve and write the answers on the lines below.

Will has 224 kayaks. He has rented 126 of them to a group of vacationers. How many kayaks have not been rented?

____ ◯ ____ = ____

Josh is picking apples from the orchard. He has picked 381 red ones and 160 green ones. How many apples does he have to make some apple pies?

____ ◯ ____ = ____

Jen and Rob took a lot of photos on vacation. Jen took 371 photos. Rob took 102 fewer photos than Jen. How many photos did Rob take?

____ ◯ ____ = ____

Alonzo sent postcards from Italy. He sent 216 postcards to friends and 116 to family members. How many postcards did he send while he was on vacation?

____ ◯ ____ = ____

Multiplication

Multiplication Using a Model

Use the groups to help solve the multiplication equations. Write the products on the lines below.

How many flowers are there?

How many flowers are in each pot? How many pots are there?

___2___ flowers in each pot x ___2___ pots

___2___ x ___2___ = ___4___

How much money is there?

How much is each coin worth? How many coins are there?

_____ cents x _____ coins

_____ x _____ = _____

Circle the groups and multiply. Write the answers on the lines below.

4 groups of grasshoppers
x ___3___ in each group.
___4___ x ___3___ = ___12___

6 groups of inchworms
x _____ in each group.
_____ x _____ = _____

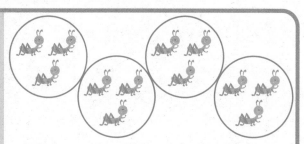

2 groups of dragonflies
x _____ in each group.
_____ x _____ = _____

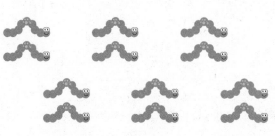

151

Relate Addition to Multiplication Using Repeated Addition

You can use repeated addition to help you solve multiplication equations.

Example: There are 3 trees in the orchard.
Each tree has 4 apples.

4   +   4   +   4   =   12

3 x 4 = 12

Look at the groups in each of the illustrations below and use repeated addition to help you solve the multiplication equation.

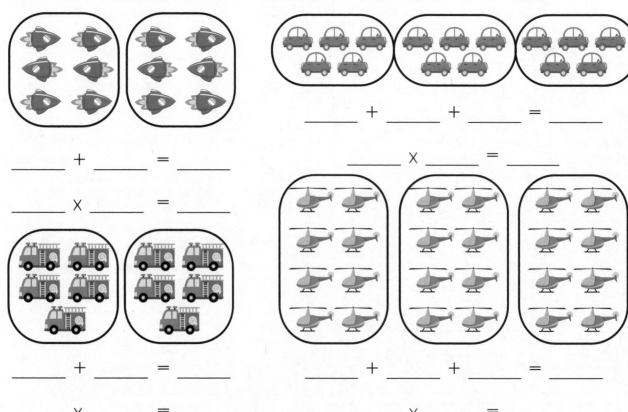

____ + ____ + ____ = ____

____ x ____ = ____

____ + ____ = ____

____ x ____ = ____

____ + ____ = ____

____ x ____ = ____

____ + ____ + ____ = ____

____ x ____ = ____

Multiplication

Identity Property and Zero Property

The zero property of multiplication says that the product of 0 multiplied by any number is 0.

Example: $1 \times 0 = 0$ and $2 \times 0 = 0$

Solve the multiplication problems and write the answers in the boxes below.

3 x 0 = ☐

10 x 0 = ☐

4 x 0 = ☐

7 x 0 = ☐

2 x 0 = ☐

5 x 0 = ☐

8 x 0 = ☐

1 x 0 = ☐

6 x 0 = ☐

9 x 0 = ☐

The identity property of multiplication says that the product of 1 multiplied by any number is that number.

Example: $3 \times 1 = 3$ and $4 \times 1 = 4$

Solve the multiplication problems and write the answers in the boxes below.

3 x 1 = ☐

9 x 1 = ☐

6 x 1 = ☐

8 x 1 = ☐

2 x 1 = ☐

5 x 1 = ☐

7 x 1 = ☐

1 x 1 = ☐

4 x 1 = ☐

10 x 1 = ☐

Multiplication

Multiplication Table

This is a multiplication table.

You can use a multiplication table to help you multiply. Move your finger along the top row to choose the number of groups you have to multiply and then move another finger down the left column to the number you have in each group. Then move your fingers down the column and across the row until they meet. The number where your fingers meet is the product!

X	0	1	2	3	4	5	6	7	8	9	10	11	12
0	0	0	0	0	0	0	0	0	0	0	0	0	0
1	0	1	2	3	4	5	6	7	8	9	10	11	12
2	0	2	4	6	8	10	12	14	16	18	20	22	24
3	0	3	6	9	12	15	18	21	24	27	30	33	36
4	0	4	8	12	16	20	24	28	32	36	40	44	48
5	0	5	10	15	20	25	30	35	40	45	50	55	60
6	0	6	12	18	24	30	36	42	48	54	60	66	72
7	0	7	14	21	28	35	42	49	56	63	70	77	84
8	0	8	16	24	32	40	48	56	64	72	80	88	96
9	0	9	18	27	36	45	54	63	72	81	90	99	108
10	0	10	20	30	40	50	60	70	80	90	100	110	120
11	0	11	22	33	44	55	66	77	88	99	110	121	132
12	0	12	24	36	48	60	72	84	96	108	120	132	144

Multiplication

Find Unknowns

A letter can be used in place of an unknown factor. When a letter is used, it is known as a variable because its value varies when used in different equations. Use the multiplication table on page 154 to help you solve for the variable.

Example:

$$n \times 4 = 12$$

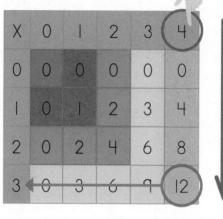

$$n = 3$$

$s \times 5 = 15$

_____ x 5 = 15

$r \times 2 = 12$

_____ x 2 = 12

$8 \times g = 56$

8 x _____ = 56

$7 \times p = 70$

7 x _____ = 70

$9 \times 9 = f$

9 x 9 = _____

$8 \times 10 = h$

8 x 10 = _____

$5 \times y = 45$

5 x _____ = 45

$r \times 7 = 77$

_____ x 7 = 77

$s \times 9 = 36$

_____ x 9 = 36

$8 \times p = 72$

8 x _____ = 72

$6 \times 4 = z$

6 x 4 = _____

$12 \times w = 84$

12 x _____ = 84

Multiplication

Commutative Property

The commutative property of multiplication states that if you flip the order of the factors, the product will stay the same.

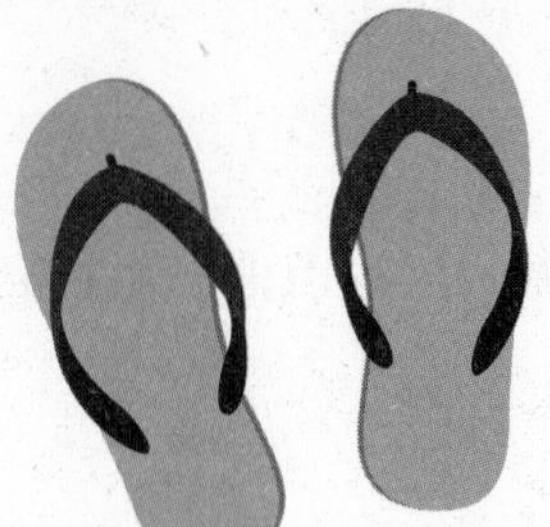

Example: 2 x 3 = 6 is the same as 3 x 2 = 6

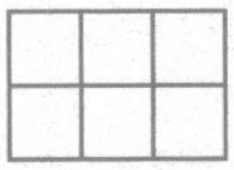

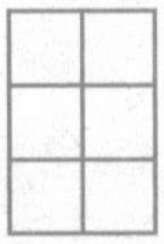

Draw a small picture in the box to show the commutative property of multiplication. Then fill in the equation to solve.

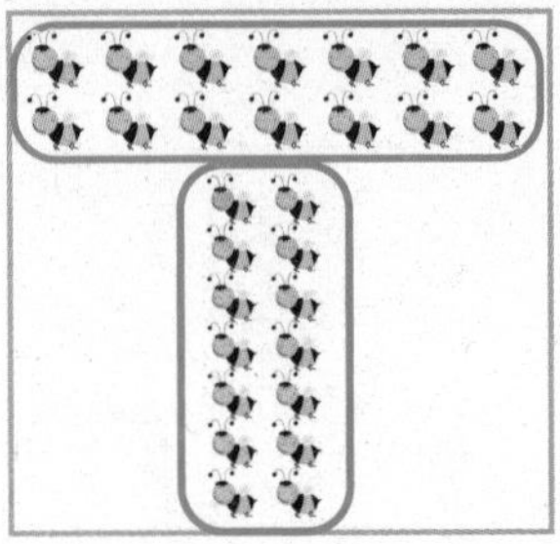

7 x <u>2</u> = 14	___ x 3 = 18	6 x 2 = ___	1 x ___ = 8
2 x <u>7</u> = 14	___ x 6 = 18	2 x ___ = 12	8 x ___ = 8

Associative Property

The associative property of multiplication states that when you have three or more factors, if the grouping of the factors changes, the product will stay the same. Use parentheses to group the factors.

Associate means who I am with.

Example: (2 x 3) x 5 = 2 x (3 x 5)

HINT: The factors didn't change. You still see 2, 3, and 5.

Use the associative property of multiplication to rewrite the equation another way. Then solve the multiplication equation.

3 x (2 x 2) =
(3 x 2) x 2 =
12

4 x (1 x 3) =
____
____

(2 x 6) x 2 =
____
____

(1 x 7) x 5 =
____
____

5 x (3 x 1) =
____
____

(6 x 3) x 2 =
____
____

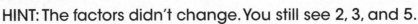

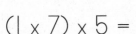

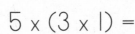

Multiplication

Arrays

You can create an array to help you solve multiplication equations. An array is a set that shows equal groups in rows and columns. By building an array, you can easily count the units to tell how many there are in all.

Example:

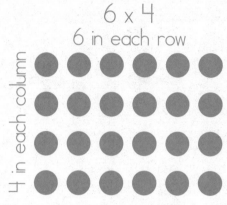

Look at the equations below. Color in the grid to show the number of rows and the number of units in each column. Then color in the grid to show how many are in each row. Solve the equation and write the products on the lines.

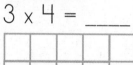

3 x 4 = _____

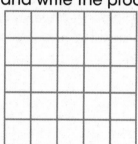

5 x 3 = _____

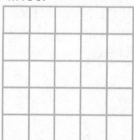

2 x 4 = _____

5 x 1 = _____

4 x 5 = _____

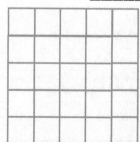

2 x 3 = _____

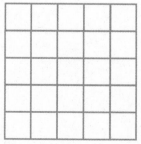

1 x 4 = _____

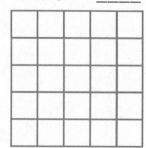

2 x 5 = _____

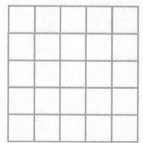

5 x 5 = _____

157

Distributive Property Using Arrays

You can use the distributive property to break apart a multiplication equation with larger numbers into two smaller equations. By solving the two smaller equations and adding the products together, you will solve the larger equation.

Example:

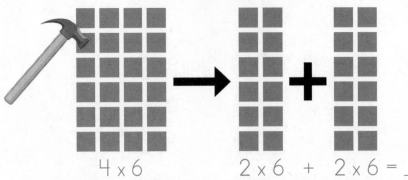

4 x 6

HINT: The number of rows stays the same.

2 x 6 + 2 x 6 = ____

Make the number in each row smaller.

Use orange to color in the square units to represent the multiplication equation. Use red to draw a line to break the array into two smaller pieces. Write the two multiplication equations you made based on your drawn red line in the parentheses below each grid. Solve by adding together the products and write your answer on the lines.

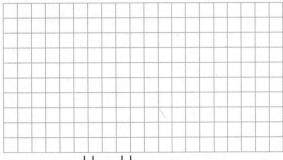

4 x 4 = ____

(4 x ____) + (4 x ____)

____ + ____ = ____

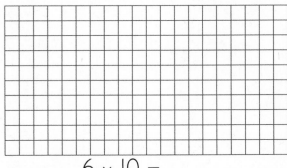

6 x 10 = ____

(6 x ____) + (6 x ____)

____ + ____ = ____

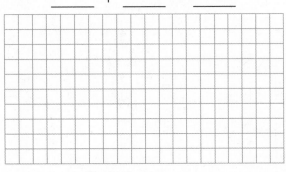

8 x 8 = ____

(8 x ____) + (8 x ____)

____ + ____ = ____

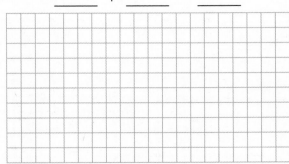

7 x 6 = ____

(7 x ____) + (7 x ____)

____ + ____ = ____

Mixed Multiplication Practice

Practice multiplying by writing the products on the lines below.

3 x 6 = _____

2 x 7 = _____

4 x 2 = _____

8 x 7 = _____

5 x 6 = _____

9 x 6 = _____

3 x 7 = _____

8 x 2 = _____

9 x 1 = _____

7 x 10 = _____

7 x 3 = _____

10 x 4 = _____

10 x 9 = _____

5 x 5 = _____

3 x 3 = _____

4 x 5 = _____

5 x 8 = _____

9 x 8 = _____

9 x 2 = _____

7 x 0 = _____

159

Multiplying by Two and Three

Solve the multiplication equations and write the products in the boxes below. Use the multiplication table on page 154 if you need help.

10 x 2 = ☐

3 x 2 = ☐

4 x 2 = ☐

7 x 2 = ☐

2 x 2 = ☐

5 x 2 = ☐

8 x 2 = ☐

1 x 2 = ☐

6 x 2 = ☐

9 x 2 = ☐

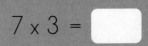

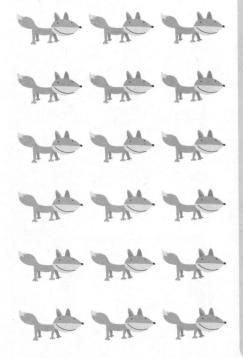

3 x 3 = ☐

9 x 3 = ☐

6 x 3 = ☐

8 x 3 = ☐

2 x 3 = ☐

5 x 3 = ☐

7 x 3 = ☐

1 x 3 = ☐

4 x 3 = ☐

10 x 3 = ☐

Multiplication

Multiplying by Four and Five

Solve the multiplication equations and write the products in the boxes below. Use the multiplication table on page 154 if you need help.

3 x 4 =

10 x 4 =

4 x 4 =

7 x 4 =

2 x 4 =

5 x 4 =

8 x 4 =

1 x 4 =

6 x 4 =

9 x 4 =

3 x 5 =

9 x 5 =

6 x 5 =

8 x 5 =

2 x 5 =

5 x 5 =

7 x 5 =

1 x 5 =

4 x 5 =

10 x 5 =

Multiplication

Multiplying by Six and Seven

Solve the multiplication equations and write the products in the boxes below. Use the multiplication table on page 154 if you need help.

$3 \times 6 =$ ☐

$10 \times 6 =$ ☐

$4 \times 6 =$ ☐

$7 \times 6 =$ ☐

$2 \times 6 =$ ☐

$5 \times 6 =$ ☐

$8 \times 6 =$ ☐

$1 \times 6 =$ ☐

$6 \times 6 =$ ☐

$9 \times 6 =$ ☐

$3 \times 7 =$ ☐

$9 \times 7 =$ ☐

$6 \times 7 =$ ☐

$8 \times 7 =$ ☐

$2 \times 7 =$ ☐

$5 \times 7 =$ ☐

$7 \times 7 =$ ☐

$1 \times 7 =$ ☐

$4 \times 7 =$ ☐

$10 \times 7 =$ ☐

Multiplication

Multiplying by Eight and Nine

Solve the multiplication equations and write the products in the boxes below. Use the multiplication table on page 154 if you need help.

$3 \times 8 =$ ☐

$10 \times 8 =$ ☐

$4 \times 8 =$ ☐

$7 \times 8 =$ ☐

$2 \times 8 =$ ☐

$5 \times 8 =$ ☐

$8 \times 8 =$ ☐

$1 \times 8 =$ ☐

$6 \times 8 =$ ☐

$9 \times 8 =$ ☐

$3 \times 9 =$ ☐

$9 \times 9 =$ ☐

$6 \times 9 =$ ☐

$8 \times 9 =$ ☐

$2 \times 9 =$ ☐

$5 \times 9 =$ ☐

$7 \times 9 =$ ☐

$1 \times 9 =$ ☐

$4 \times 9 =$ ☐

$10 \times 9 =$ ☐

Multiplication

Multiplication Word Problems

When solving word problems, look for clues. Numbers and words are clues! Circle the numbers in the word problems and look for word clues. Hint: When a word problem has multiple groups to add, it means multiply.

Example: Rory walks ②miles to school every day. She goes to school ⑤ times a week. How many miles does she walk in a school week?

$$2 \times 5 = 10 \text{ miles}$$

Circle the clues and solve the word problems. Write the products on the lines below.

Lorelai loves pickles. She eats 2 pickles 3 times a day. How many pickles does she eat every day?

____ x ____ = ____

Kirk owns 5 pairs of sunglasses. Patty owns 2 times that amount. How many pairs of sunglasses does Patty own?

____ x ____ = ____

Richard bought 4 boxes of cakes. Each box has 4 cakes in it. How many total cakes does Richard have?

____ x ____ = ____

Emily eats 3 bunches of grapes. Each bunch has 10 grapes. How many grapes did Emily eat?

____ x ____ = ____

Division

Exploring Division

Dividing **means** separating things into smaller groups.

Example: **There are** 8 hats altogether.

They are placed into 2 equal groups.

8 hats divided into 2 groups equals 4 hats in each group.

8 ÷ 2 = 4

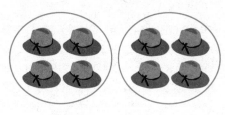

Circle the objects and answer the questions to divide. Write the answers on the lines below.

How many shoes are there altogether? __10__
Place the shoes into groups of 2 by circling equal sets.
How many groups are there? __5__
10 ÷ 2 = __5__

How many flowers are there altogether? _____
Place the flowers into groups of 3 by circling equal sets.
How many groups are there? _____
12 ÷ 3 = ____

How many gloves are there altogether? _____
Place the gloves into groups of 4 by circling equal sets.
How many groups are there? _____
20 ÷ 4 = ____

How many bows are there altogether? _____
Place the bows into groups of 5 by circling equal sets.
How many groups are there? _____
15 ÷ 5 = ____

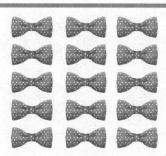

165

Division

Exploring Division

You can use an array to help you solve a division problem. In division you start with the whole set, known as the dividend. The divisor is one part of the dividend. The quotient is the answer (and the other part of the dividend). Use the arrays below to help solve the problems. Write the quotients on the lines below.

How many apples are there altogether?_____

Place the apples into groups of 2 by circling equal sets.

How many groups are there? _____

12 ÷ 2 = _____

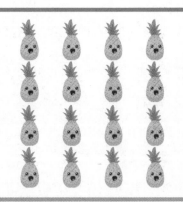

How many bananas are there altogether?_____

Place the bananas into groups of 3 by circling equal sets.

How many groups are there? _____

15 ÷ 3 = _____

How many pineapples are there altogether?_____

Place the pineapples into groups of 4 by circling equal sets.

How many groups are there? _____

16 ÷ 4 = _____

How many watermelons are there altogether?_____

Place the watermelons into groups of 5 by circling equal sets.

How many groups are there? _____

10 ÷ 5 = _____

Fact Families

Just like subtraction is related to addition, multiplication is related to division. You can use multiplication-related facts to help you solve division.

Example: If I know that 5 x 6 = 30, then 30 ÷ 5 = 6

Use related facts and the properties of multiplication to help you fill in the multiplication and division fact families.

4 x __5__ = 20	____ x 6 = 24
__5__ x 4 = 20	6 x ____ = 24
20 ÷ 4 = __5__	24 ÷ 6 = ____
20 ÷ __5__ = 4	24 ÷ ____ = 6
9 x ____ = 27	5 x ____ = 10
____ x 9 = 27	____ x 5 = 10
27 ÷ 9 = ____	10 ÷ 5 = ____
27 ÷ ____ = 9	10 ÷ ____ = 5
2 x ____ = 14	4 x ____ = 28
____ x 7 = 14	____ x 7 = 28
14 ÷ 7 = ____	28 ÷ 7 = ____
14 ÷ ____ = 7	28 ÷ ____ = 7

Division

Division Word Problems

Circle the groups to help you divide. Then solve the division word problems and write the quotients on the lines below.

Annie has 8 flowerpots to give to her 4 friends.

How many flowerpots will each friend get?

8 ÷ 4 = __2__

Pat has 15 books to put into 3 boxes.
How many books will go into each box?

15 ÷ 3 = _____

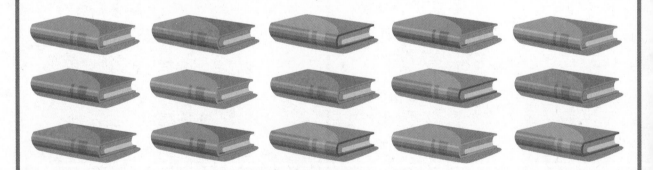

Katie has 12 cookies on a plate. She wants to share them equally with 4 friends. How many cookies will each friend get?

12 ÷ 4 = _____

Fractions

Fractions

Fractions **are** parts of a whole number. **Each piece represents a part of the whole.**

Example: If a cookie is cut into two equal parts, each piece is $\frac{1}{2}$ of the whole cookie.

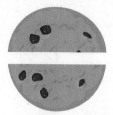

Fractions are expressed as a part over a whole. The part on top is known as the numerator. The numerator tells how many parts are shaded. The bottom number is known as the denominator. The denominator tells how many parts there are in the whole.

Example:

$$= \frac{1}{4} \quad \frac{\text{numerator}}{\text{denominator}}$$

The 1 represents how many parts are shaded.

The 4 represents how many parts there are in the whole shape.

Write the missing numerators or denominators for the fractions shown below.

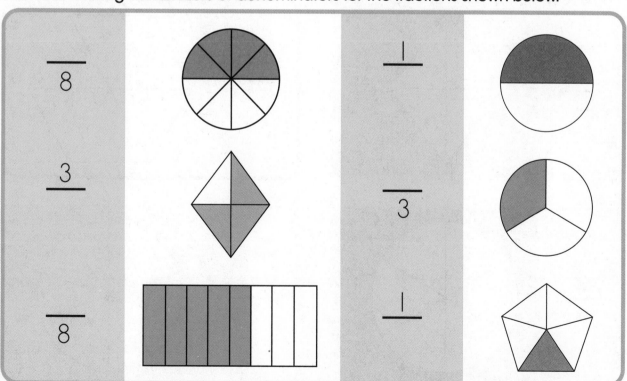

Fractions

Color the parts of the shapes to match the fractions.

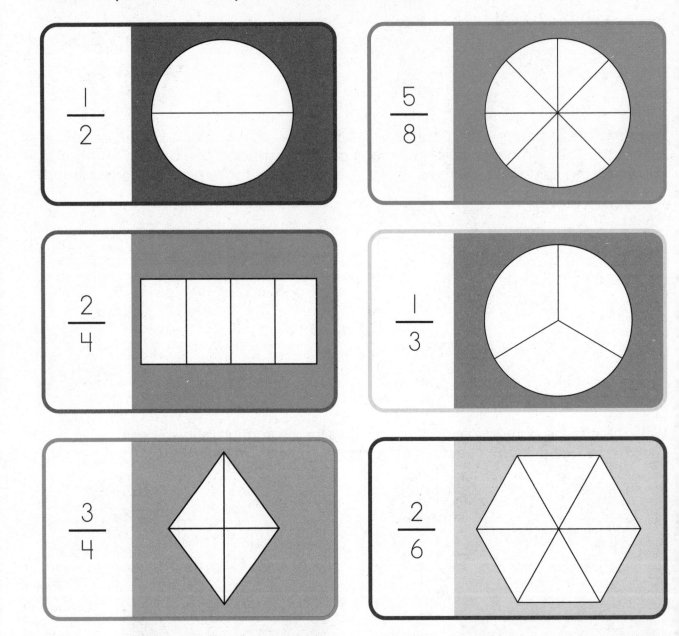

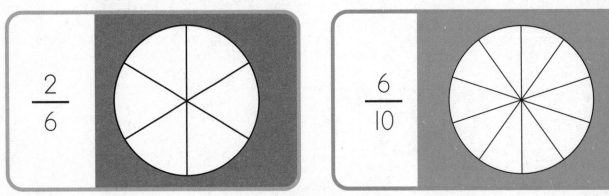

Fractions

Fractions on a Number Line

You can use a number line to show fractions. The length or distance from one whole number to the next whole number represents one whole. The number line can be broken into any number of equal parts.

Example: Drew's family is traveling from his house to his aunt May's farm. They stop at a gas station when they are $\frac{3}{4}$ of the way there.

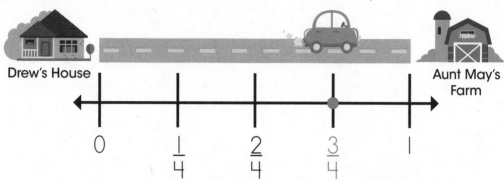

Drew's House   Aunt May's Farm

$$0 \qquad \frac{1}{4} \qquad \frac{2}{4} \qquad \frac{3}{4} \qquad 1$$

$\frac{3}{4}$ is 3 out of 4 equal parts. By counting forward 3 parts starting with 0, you can mark the fraction on the number line.

Break each number line below into equal parts based on each fraction's denominator. Write each fraction on the number line and then place a dot on the correct fraction. HINT: The denominator, or bottom number, tells you how many equal parts there will be in all.

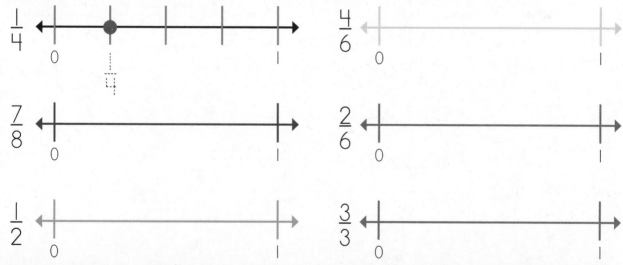

If a number line is partitioned into eighths, how many equal parts are there? ____

If a number line is partitioned into fourths, how many equal parts are there? ____

Fractions

Fractions on a Number Line

Look at the number lines below to answer the questions.

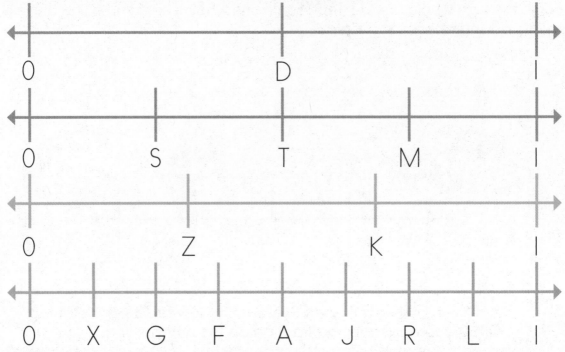

What letter represents 2/3? _____

What letter represents 3/4? _____

What letter represents 2/8? _____

What letter represents 1/4? _____

What letter represents 7/8? _____

What letter represents 1/8? _____

What letter represents 2/4? _____

Which 3 letters are equal to 1/2 on the number line?

_____ _____ _____

Which letter is equal to 6/8? _____

Put a dot on 4/4 on the number line with four equal parts.

Compare Fractions

Just like you can compare whole numbers, you can also compare fractions.

Example: Sue ate 3/6 of her cookie, and Bob ate 5/6 of his cookie. Who ate more of their cookie?

Sue's Cookie

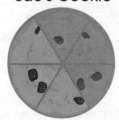

Bob ate more of his cookie than Sue.

3/6 < 5/6

Bob's Cookie

Color in the shapes to match the fractions. Then look at the fractions and use <, >, or = to compare the two "parts to whole" amounts.

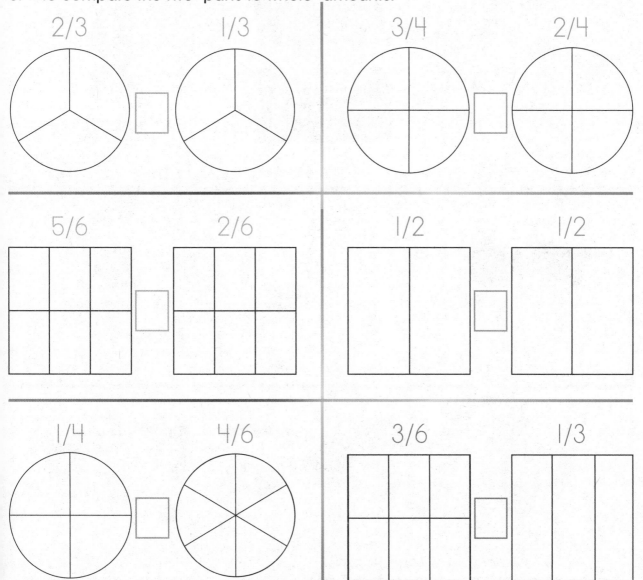

2/3   1/3

3/4   2/4

5/6   2/6

1/2   1/2

1/4   4/6

3/6   1/3

Measuring Length

An inch can be written like this: in.
It is used to measure short lengths.

A foot can be written like this: ft.
It is used to measure longer lengths.

A mile can be written like this: mi.
It is used to measure very long lengths.

An estimate is a thoughtful guess. Sometimes we need to make a thoughtful guess about how long something is.

Look at the pictures below and circle the unit of measurement that would be the best for measuring each REAL object.

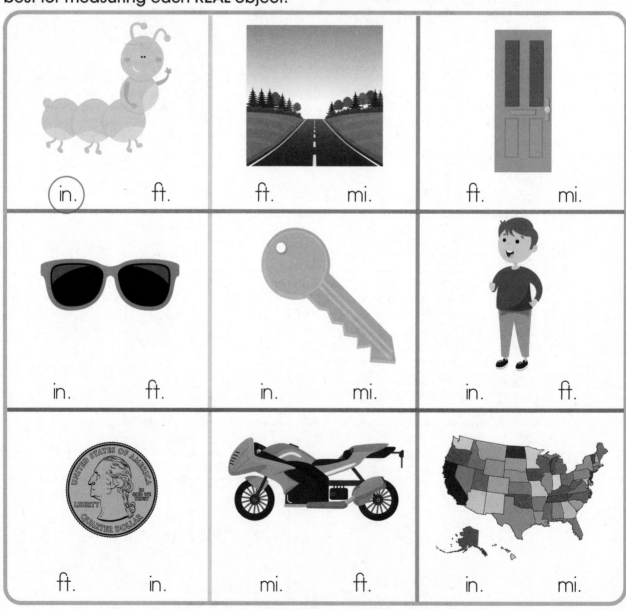

(in.) ft.	ft. mi.	ft. mi.
in. ft.	in. mi.	in. ft.
ft. in.	mi. ft.	in. mi.

Measuring Length

Measure the objects using the ruler. Write the measured lengths on the lines below.

_____ in.

_____ in.

_____ in.

Read the word problems and circle or write the answers below.

Stacia wants to measure the length of her book. Which measurement is best for her to use?

      in.   mi.   ft.

Chad threw a baseball 9 feet. His friend Carol threw it 4 more feet than Chad. How far did they throw the ball altogether?

_____ ft. + _____ ft. = _____ ft.

Lauren wants to measure the height of the tree in her yard. Which measurement is best for her to use?

      in.   mi.   ft.

Capacity

If you want to know how much a container holds (for example, how much water a swimming pool can hold), you want to know its capacity.

A liter can be written like this: L.

It is used to measure large containers, such as a pool or a bathtub.

A milliliter can be written like this: mL.

It is used to measure small containers, such as a spoon or measuring cup.

1 liter = 1000 milliliters   and $\frac{1}{2}$ liter = 500 milliliters

Color each container to the correct measurement in milliliters.

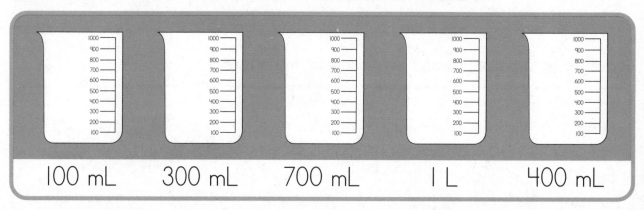

| 100 mL | 300 mL | 700 mL | 1 L | 400 mL |

Do these containers hold more or less than a liter? Check the box with the correct answer for each container.

	more than / less than		more than / less than
	more than / less than		more than / less than

Capacity

You can use what you know about fractions to measure capacities.

Example:

$\frac{1}{4}$ (1 quarter) $\frac{1}{2}$ (1 half) $\frac{3}{4}$ (3 quarters)   full

Color each of the glasses with a yellow colored pencil to give each person the amount of lemonade he or she wants.

David wants three quarters of a glass of lemonade.

Colleen wants a half glass of lemonade.

Carol wants a quarter of a glass of lemonade.

Isaiah wants a full glass of lemonade.

Word Problem

If a plastic pool holds 20 liters of water, how many 5 liter buckets of water will you need to use to fill it up?

 ÷ _____ = _____

20 liters   5 liters

Measurement

Mass

Mass is a measurement of how much matter is in an object. Mass is measured in kilograms (kg) or grams (g). Kilograms measure objects with larger masses. Grams measure objects with smaller masses.

Example: The mass of a kitten is about 2 kg.

The mass of a diamond ring is about 1.5 g.

The mass of an apple is about 100 g.

If both things on either end of a scale have the same mass, the scale will balance. Write the mass of the food items in the boxes below.

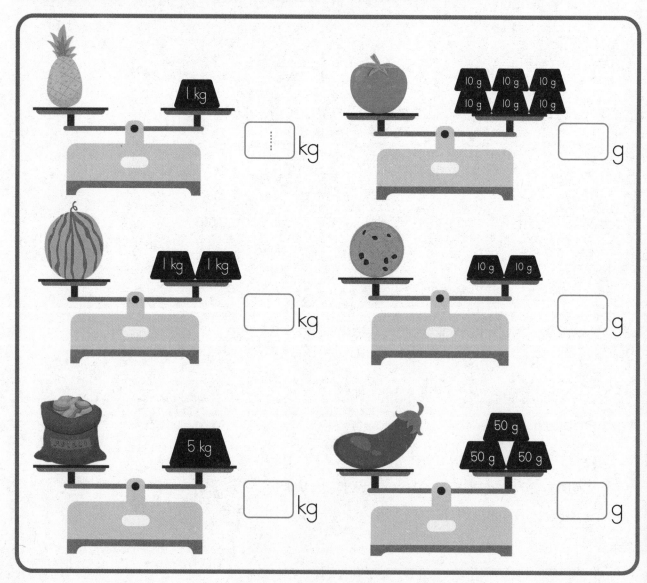

Time

Time to the Minute

The minute hand tells how many minutes have passed in an hour. In 1 minute, the minute hand moves from one hash mark to the next. Every time the minute hand moves from one whole number to the next, it has been 5 minutes. Skip count by fives and then count forward one for each hash mark to tell how many minutes after the hour have passed.

Example: The hour hand is past 3 but not yet near 4. The minute hand is 2 marks past 15, so it is 3:17.

What time is it? Write the time under each clock.

2:23

What time is it? Draw the hands on the clocks to match the digital times.

5:07   3:59   6:16

179

Time

A.M. and P.M.

Writing a.m. or p.m. after a time lets you know if it is daytime or nighttime. You use a.m. for anytime from midnight to midday, or noon. You use p.m. for anytime from midday, or noon, until midnight. You can use a number line to think about time as distance. It can also help you think about the number of hours in a day. There are twelve hours in the a.m. and twelve hours in the p.m. A day is twenty-four hours altogether!

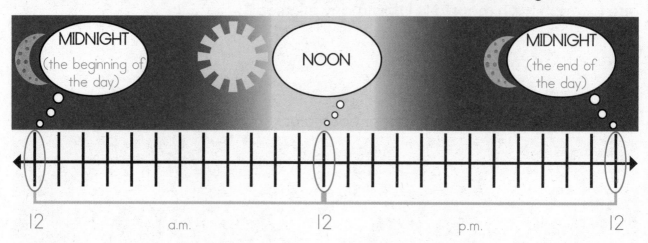

Think about the activities and the time on the clock. Then write the time for the activity on the lines below using a.m. or p.m.

Ride a bicycle _____   Eat dinner _____   Make eggs _____

Go to bed _____   Go to school _____   Play baseball _____

Quarter after 8 in the morning 8:15 a.m.

8 minutes after 7 in the evening 7:08 p.m.

AJ has practice 22 minutes after 4 in the afternoon. _____

Luca eats breakfast at half past 7 in the morning. _____

Nolen leaves for school 25 minutes before 8 in the morning. _____

Huxley feeds Pepper at quarter after 5 in the evening. _____

Time

Elapsed Time

Elapsed time **means** how much time has passed. You can use a number line to help you figure out elapsed time.

Example: Ashton started baseball practice at 4:30 p.m. His practice ended at 6:15 p.m. How long was Ashton's practice? **HINT: There are 60 minutes in an hour.**

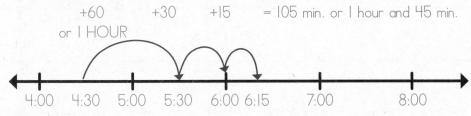

Read each word problem carefully. Use the number line to help you figure out the elapsed time. Start by creating the hash marks you need to represent the hours in the span of time. Then draw your arrows and write the amount of elapsed time on the lines below.

 Sarah started her homework at 3:15 p.m. She finished all of her homework at 4:30 p.m. How long did it take Sarah to finish her homework? _____

Kelly went to the mall at 10:30 a.m. She got home at 12:15 p.m. How long did Kelly shop at the mall?

_____

 Morgan went for a run. He left the house at 5:25 a.m. Morgan finished his run at 7:20 a.m. How long did he run this morning? _____

181

Reading a Scaled Bar Graph

Reading a scaled bar graph means counting the numbers each bar represents and analyzing the data. Scaled bar graphs mean that the number of each unit of measure will represent more than one. In the graph below, the scale increment is by fives.

Look at the scaled bar graph and answer the questions. Write the answers on the lines below.

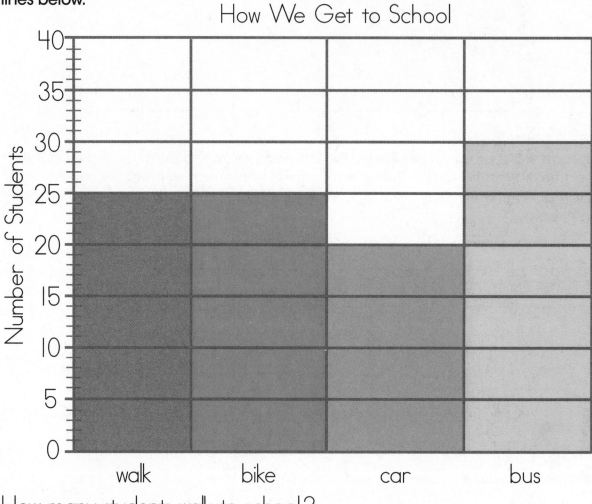

How many students walk to school? _____

How many students ride their bikes to school? _____

Do more students take the bus or ride in a car? _____

How many students altogether walk or ride their bikes? _____

What is the most popular way to get to school? _____

What is the least popular way to get to school? _____

Data Management

Making a Scaled Bar Graph

Use the tally graph data to make a scaled bar graph. Then answer the questions.
Write the answers on the lines below.

jumping rope	ⅢⅣ ⅢⅣ II
playing sports	ⅢⅣ ⅢⅣ ⅢⅣ ⅢⅣ
reading a book	ⅢⅣ ⅢⅣ IIII
talking with friends	ⅢⅣ III
swinging	II

Recess Fun

(bar graph: Number of Students vs. jumping rope, playing sports, reading a book, talking with friends, swinging; y-axis 2–22)

How many kids like jumping rope at recess? _____

How many kids like reading a book? _____

What is the most popular recess activity? _____

What is the least popular recess activity? _____

How many kids voted altogether? _____

Congruent Shapes

Congruent shapes are figures that are the same size and same shape.

Are the shapes below congruent? Circle yes or no.

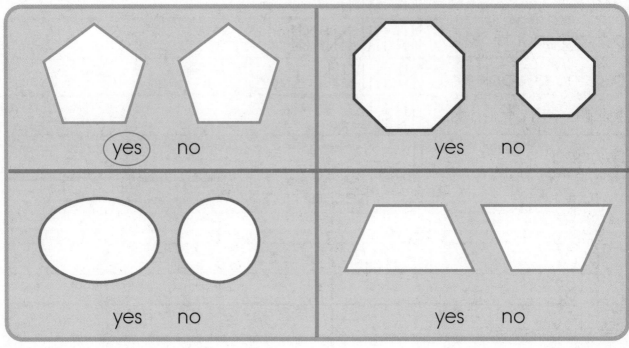

yes   no   yes   no

yes   no   yes   no

Color the congruent figures orange.

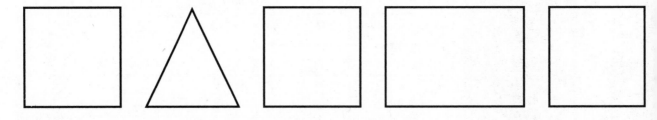

Draw two figures that are congruent in the box below.

Geometry

Plane Figures

A plane figure is a figure that is formed on a flat surface. It is formed by points that make line segments, curved paths, or both.

Example: A point marks an exact location.

Endpoints are used to show segments of a line.

A line segment is straight, a part of a line and has two endpoints.

A line is a straight path that continues in both directions and does not end.

A ray is straight, part of a line, has one end point, and continues on in one direction.

A curved path will have a bend in its line.

A closed shape starts and ends at the same point.

An open shape does not start and end at the same point.

Write how many line segments each figure has on the lines below.

    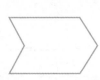   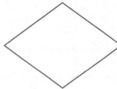   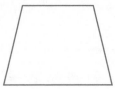   

_____   _____   _____   _____   _____

Look at the figures below and write whether the figures are open or closed.

    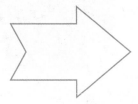   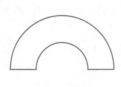

_____   _____   _____   _____   _____

185

Geometry

Angles

An angle is formed when two line segments share the same endpoint. A right angle is an angle that forms a square corner. Some angles can be less than a right angle, and some angles can be greater than a right angle.

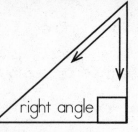

Use the corner of a piece of paper to help you determine whether the angles on the figures below are right angles, less than right angles, or greater than right angles. Write your answer on the lines.

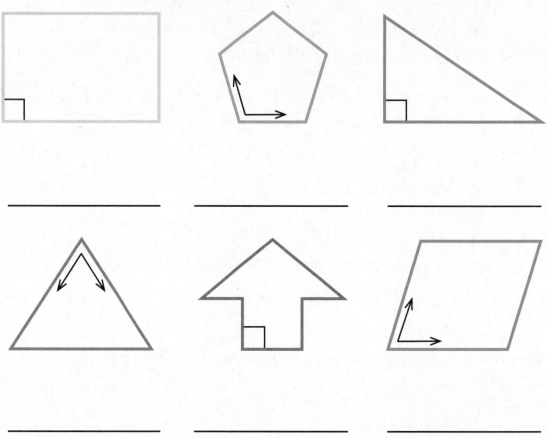

_____   _____   _____

_____   _____   _____

Look at the shapes below. Write how many right angles each shape has on the lines below.

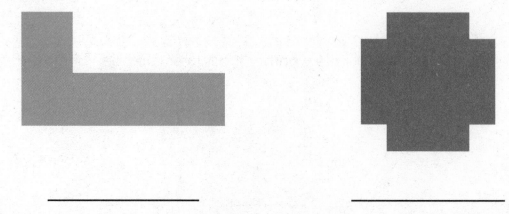

_____   _____

Geometry

Identifying Polygons

A polygon is any two-dimensional figure with three or more sides. That means there are a lot of different kinds of polygons!

Oftentimes, a figure is named for the number of sides and number of angles it has in total.

Example: A triangle has 3 sides and angles.   "Tri" means three.

A quadrilateral has 4 sides and angles. "Quad" means four.

A pentagon has 5 sides and angles.   "Penta" means five.

A hexagon has 6 sides and angles.   "Hexa" means six.

A heptagon has 7 sides and angles.   "Hepta" means seven.

An octagon has 8 sides and angles.   "Octa" means eight.

Write how many sides and angles each polygon has on the lines below.

  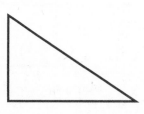

____ sides   ____ sides   ____ sides

____ angles   ____ angles   ____ angles

Perimeter

Perimeter is the distance around a figure. If you walked along an entire fence surrounding a horse in a field, you could say, "I walked the perimeter, and now I am tired!"

Example: What is the fence perimeter around the horse in this field? You can find the perimeter by adding together the length of each side. The rectangular fence has four sides.

A rectangle has two sides that are parallel and the same length. In order to find the perimeter, you need to add the two missing side lengths.

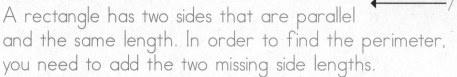

Add 4 ft. + 7 ft. + 4 ft. + 7 ft. = 22 ft.

11 ft. + 11 ft. = 22 ft.

The fence perimeter is 22 feet long.

Fill in the missing lengths and then find the perimeter of each figure. Be sure to include the units in your answer.

6 yd · 2 yd rectangle

Perimeter: _____

2 in. · 9 in. rectangle

Perimeter: _____

3 ft. · 5 ft. rectangle

Perimeter: _____

HINT: A square has four sides that are all the same length.

4 in. square

Perimeter: _____

10 ft. · 6 ft. rectangle

Perimeter: _____

2 in. · 2 in. square

Perimeter: _____

Solve the perimeter word problems below. Write your answers on the lines.

A rectangle has a side that is 5 inches long and a side that is 7 inches long. What is the perimeter of the rectangle? _____

A square has a side that is 8 feet long. What is the perimeter of the square? _____

Perimeter

Polygon Perimeters

Find the perimeter of the polygons below. Remember that to find the perimeter, you need to add each side of the polygon together.

Find the perimeter of the figures below. Be sure to include the units in your answer.

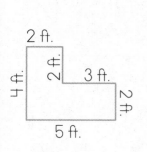

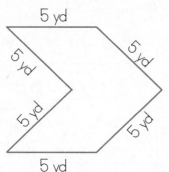

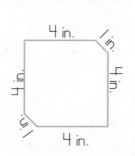

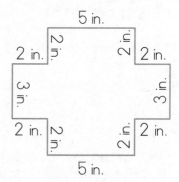

Perimeter: _____

Perimeter: _____

Perimeter: _____

Perimeter: _____

Look at the figures. Find the unknown side lengths.

Perimeter = 16 ft.

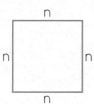

n = _____

Perimeter = 32 ft.

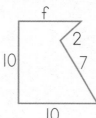

f = _____

Perimeter = 18 ft.

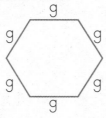

g = _____

Perimeter = 24 ft.

x = _____

Solve the perimeter word problems below. Write your answers on the lines.

A pencil case has a height of 7 inches and a width of 4 inches. What is the perimeter of the pencil case?_____

Ellie got an envelope in the mail. It had a height of 8 inches and a width of 5 inches. What is the perimeter of the envelope?____

189

Area

You have learned that perimeter is the distance around a figure. Area is the measurement of the number of square units used to cover a surface. For example, builders need to know how many square units there are in a kitchen floor to make sure they have enough wood to cover the entire floor area.

Unit Square

Example: You can find area by counting the number of square units. This figure has an area of 3 sq. units.

Draw lines to make square units inside each figure. Then count the square units to find the area of the figures below. Write the answer on the lines.

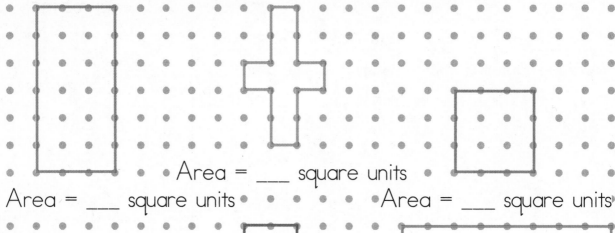

Area = ___ square units

Area = ___ square units

Area = ___ square units

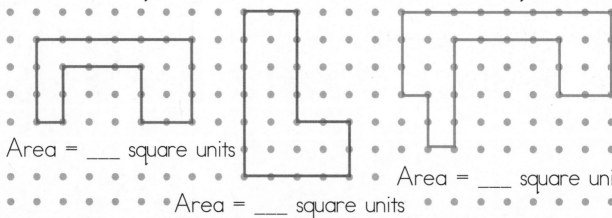

Area = ___ square units

Area = ___ square units

Area = ___ square units

Write area or perimeter for each situation.

Carpeting a floor

_____

Putting tile on a bathroom wall

_____

Fencing a garden

_____

Enclosing a playground in a backyard

_____

190

Area

Relate Multiplication to Area

A more efficient way to find the area of a figure is by using multiplication. You can use what you know about arrays in multiplication to help you figure out the area.

Example: This rectangle is like an array.

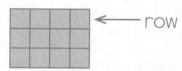 ← row

   1. Count the number of rows. __3__

   2. Count how many units are in each row. __4__

You can now multiply how many square units are in each row by the number of rows.

$3 \times 4 = 12$, so the area of this rectangle is 12 square units.

Find the area of the figures below. Write the multiplication equation and the area on the lines.

____ x ____ = ____   ____ x ____ = ____   ____ x ____ = ____

Area = ____ sq. units   Area = ____ sq. units   Area = ____ sq. units

The city is planning a new park. The area for the playground is 8 units wide by 4 units long. How many square units is the area for the playground?

_____ square units

Greg helps his dad build a chicken coop that is 6 yards long by 2 yards wide. How many square yards long will the chicken coop be?

_____ square yards

Word Problems

Two-Step Word Problems

Sometimes word problems have more than one step to solve before answering the question. When reading a word problem, try to picture what is happening in your mind to help you know what different steps you need to take.

Example: Kelly went to the department store. She bought 2 shirts that cost $12 each. When Kelly started shopping, she had $42. How much money did she have left after she bought the shirts?

STEP 1: How much money did she spend on the shirts? She bought 2 shirts, and each shirt cost $12. To solve the first step, you need to add 12 + 12 or multiply 12 x 2. Kelly spent $24.

STEP 2: Kelly started with $42. If she spent money, that means you need to subtract to take that money away from her original amount of money. $42 - $24 = $18

The final answer is Kelly has $18 left after buying two shirts.

Read each word problem carefully. Complete each step that is needed and show your work. Write your answers below.

Derek had 3 packs of baseball cards. Each pack had 10 cards. He gave 8 cards to his friends. How many cards does Derek still have?

Joey baked 36 cookies. His dad ate 12 of his cookies. Joey then gave his friend some cookies. He now has 10 cookies left. How many cookies did he give his friend?

Avery has 42 markers in her box. She gave 3 friends 3 markers each. How many markers does Avery have left?

Word Problems

Two-Step Word Problems

Read each word problem carefully. Complete each step that is needed and show your work. Write your answers below.

Scott bought 4 books from the bookstore. Each book cost $5. He also bought a backpack for $8. How much money did Scott spend?

Troy made 15 bracelets. He gave 2 bracelets each to 2 friends. How many bracelets does Troy have left?

Grady has 20 toy cars. He buys 15 more cars from the store. Grady gave 6 cars to his brother. How many toy cars does Grady have now?

Ed planted a garden. He planted 3 rows of corn with 6 seeds in each row. He then planted 12 bean seeds. How many seeds did Ed plant?

Brady has 4 packs of candy. Each pack has 11 candies in it. Brady gives 10 candies to his friend. How many candies does Brady have left?

Laura has 42 beads. She makes 4 bracelets. Each bracelet has 6 beads on it. How many beads does Laura still have to make more bracelets?

CERTIFICATE
of Achievement

....

has successfully completed

3rd Grade Math

Date:

Signed:

Extra Practice Pages

Table of Contents

Practicing Sight Words

Roll a die and write the sight word that matches the number you rolled in the correct column. Roll until you fill the grid.

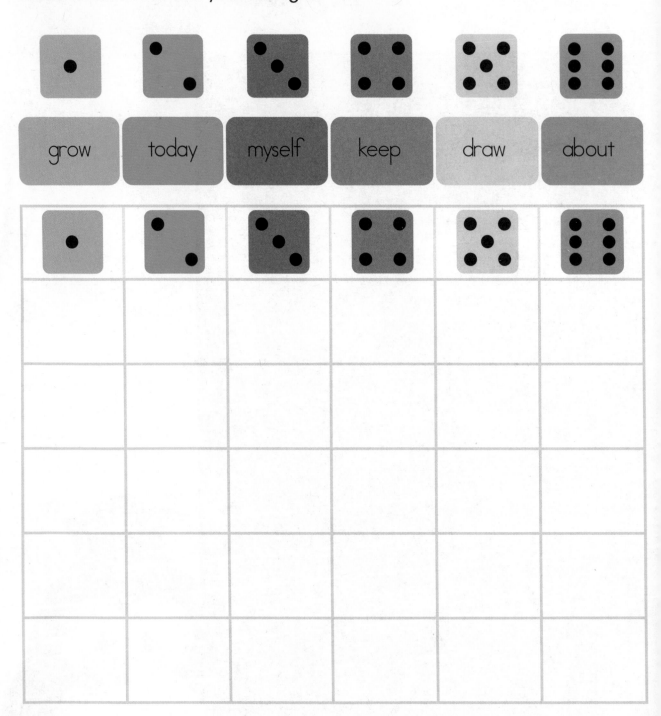

Which word filled the chart first? Write a sentence using that word on the line below.

Syllables

Read the words below out loud as you clap each syllable. How many syllables do you hear? Sort the words into the correct categories based on the number of claps you hear. Write them on the lines below.

tangerine   peach   banana   papaya   orange   lime

apple   pear   mango   cherry   lemon   strawberry

1 SYLLABLE	2 SYLLABLES	3 SYLLABLES

Using Context Clues

Read each sentence below. What does each word in red mean? Underline the words in the sentence that help you figure out the meaning of that word. Write your own definition of the word on the lines below each sentence.

That ant is miniscule. I can barely see it!

_____

_____

I was terrified when my sister put on a monster mask.

_____

_____

The librarian recommended a new book for me. He thinks I'll really like it.

_____

_____

This bug spray is not very effective. I have a lot of mosquito bites!

_____

_____

I am using a glue stick to attach a flower to my paper.

_____

_____

I don't understand the question. Can you elaborate?

_____

_____

He's very modest. He doesn't like to brag.

_____

_____

Vocabulary

Look up the words below in a dictionary. Write the definition on the lines below.

assist

_____
_____

fossil

_____
_____

absorb

_____
_____

imaginary

_____
_____

climate

_____
_____

project

_____
_____

routine

_____
_____

essential

_____
_____

Reading Comprehension

Facts and Opinions

Read each sentence below and determine if it is a fact or an opinion. Circle the correct answer.

Orange juice tastes better than apple juice.	fact	opinion
Multiplication is easier than addition.	fact	opinion
Watermelon is a type of fruit.	fact	opinion
Snow only falls when the temperature is cold enough.	fact	opinion
Plants need sunlight to grow.	fact	opinion
Reading is more fun than playing basketball.	fact	opinion
The sun is out during the day.	fact	opinion
Everybody likes broccoli.	fact	opinion
Being a chef is harder than being a doctor.	fact	opinion
Penguins can't fly.	fact	opinion
August has thirty-one days.	fact	opinion
Summer should be longer.	fact	opinion

Write one sentence that is a fact.

_____

_____

Write one sentence that is your opinion.

_____

_____

Reading Comprehension

Making Predictions

Read the sentences below and circle what you predict will come next.

I forgot to do my homework, and I...

    a. received a bad grade.   **b.** went to lunch.   **c.** got a new toy.

My dad packed me two pudding cups, so I...

    a. missed lunch.   **b.** got sent home early.   **c.** gave one to my friend.

There is a lot of snow outside, so...

    a. it must be Tuesday.   **b.** school might be canceled.   **c.** my mom will mow the lawn.

After I got a 100 on my spelling test, I felt...

    a. tired.   **b.** hungry.   **c.** happy.

If I don't take out the trash...

    a. I will see my cousins.   **b.** our house will start to smell bad.   **c.** my dog will eat her food.

Because we're going to the pool...

    a. I put on sunscreen.   **b.** I put on my winter coat.   **c.** I did laundry.

Grammar

| better | more expensive | taller | as often as |
| more | more carefully | shorter | as perfectly as |

Read each sentence below. Use the comparative adverbs in the table above to complete the sentences.

1. A gorilla eats _____ food than a cat.

2. My dad is _____ than me.

3. The cake isn't decorated _____ this one.

4. My sister is _____ at video games than I am.

5. This sweater is _____ than this coat.

6. I cut the paper _____ than last time.

7. My friend doesn't bring sandwiches for lunch _____ I do.

8. An inch is _____ than a foot.

smartest	most important	least favorite	last
funniest	most popular	least spicy	first

Read each sentence below. Use the superlative adverbs in the table above to complete the sentences.

1. The cartoon with the talking pineapple is the _____ show on TV.

2. A hamster is the _____ class pet.

3. Bell pepper is the _____ type of pepper.

4. Breakfast is the _____ meal of the day.

5. My teacher is the _____ person I know.

6. The _____ thing I do before bed is brush my teeth.

7. Oranges are my _____ fruit.

8. Our project came _____ in the science fair.

Writing Complex Sentences

For each sentence below:

- **circle the** independent clause in red
- **circle the** dependent clause in blue
- **put a box around the** subordinating conjunction in purple

My mom gave me an ice-cream cone because I got a 100 on my multiplication test.

If you come to my birthday party, we can play hide-and-seek.

Even though I'm younger than him, I'm better at board games than my brother.

I can't go to the movies unless I do my homework.

My sister packed my lunch while I tied my shoes.

Writing Sentences

Read the sentences in the blue box below. Rewrite the sentences using the dialogue rules. Hint: There will be four paragraphs. Look at page 97 if you need help remembering the dialogue rules.

> Maria gave me half of her sandwich, and she said, Can I have half of yours? Okay, I said, but then I get half of your cookie! Deal, she said. She gave me half of her cookie. I can't wait to eat this, I said, I'm starving!

Revising and Editing Writing

Read the passage. Use the checklist and proofreading marks from page 101 to help revise and edit this draft. Then draw a picture to match the passage below.

We Deserve More Recess

I think weas students disserve to have recess for an extra our on fridays. children need too be active to help exercise there growing muscles. My teacher mr Gary agrees. He told me If students don't exercise enough, they will get distacted during class." In conclusion, I think recess needs to be longer on Fridays

The Writing Process

Brainstorming

Over the next few pages, you can write about a subject of your choosing based on the types of writing you've learned in this book. You can write a narrative story, expository writing, an opinion text, procedural writing, descriptive writing, or a fable.

Use the blank box below to brainstorm for the topic you want to write about.

Time To Write

Use your brainstorming notes to write about your topic on the lines below and on the next pages. Be sure to use a variety of sentence types (simple, compound, and complex.)

Title_____

_____

_____

_____

_____

_____

_____

_____

_____

_____

_____

_____

_____

_____

_____

_____

_____

_____

_____

_____

_____

_____

_____

_____

_____

_____

_____

_____

_____

_____

cont.

cont.

_____

_____

_____

_____

_____

_____

_____

_____

_____

_____

_____

_____

_____

_____

_____

Time to Revise and Edit

Using the proofreading marks below, re-read your draft and make any necessary revisions and edits with a colored pencil or pen.

PROOFREADING MARKS

Capital Letter	Lowercase Letter	Add Comma	Add Quotation Marks	Delete
Add Period	Add Question Mark	Add Exclamation Point	sp. Spelling Error	New Paragraph
Make Space	Close Up Space	Reverse Letters/Words	Insert Word	Insert a Letter

Publishing

Rewrite your draft as a final copy using a pencil or pen, or by typing on a computer or tablet. Share your writing with your family and friends!

Least to Greatest

Put the numbers in order from least to greatest. Write the numbers on the lines below.

1,126 4,019 3,343 6,202	_____, _____, _____, _____
2,004 7,207 1,080 5,413	_____, _____, _____, _____
8,320 3,111 6,020 1,337	_____, _____, _____, _____
4,612 2,104 2,982 5,508	_____, _____, _____, _____
1,357 9,400 8,642 9,450	_____, _____, _____, _____

Use the models below to count and write how many thousands, hundreds, tens, and ones there are on the lines below.

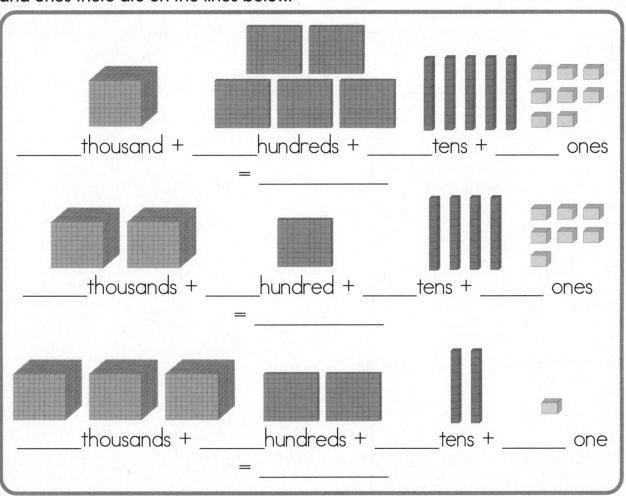

_____ thousand + _____ hundreds + _____ tens + _____ ones

= _____

_____ thousands + _____ hundred + _____ tens + _____ ones

= _____

_____ thousands + _____ hundreds + _____ tens + _____ one

= _____

Use the number line to help you round. Read the numbers and mark them on the number lines with a dot. Then round to the nearest ten and write your answers on the lines below.

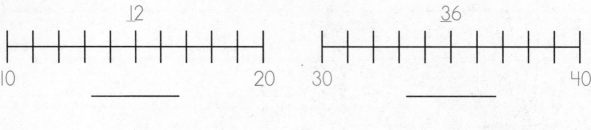

12   36

10 _____ 20   30 _____ 40

87   73

80 _____ 90   70 _____ 80

Round to the nearest ten. Write the answers on the lines.

92 _____   42 _____   28 _____   65 _____

Use the number line to help you round. Read the numbers and mark them on the number lines with a dot. Then round to the nearest hundred and write your answer on the lines below.

179   323

100 _____ 200   300 _____ 400

444   790

400 _____ 500   700 _____ 800

Round to the nearest hundred. Write the answers on the lines below.

874 _____   563 _____   218 _____   604 _____

The lion weighs 287 pounds. What is its weight rounded to the nearest hundred pounds? _____ pounds

Addition and Subtraction

Adding Three-Digit Numbers by Regrouping

Adding hundreds, tens, and ones sometimes involves regrouping. If the numbers in a column add up to more than 9, you need to regroup to the next higher place value.

Solve the problems by regrouping. Write the answers in the boxes below.

Hundreds	Tens	Ones
2	4	8
+ 1	3	5

Hundreds	Tens	Ones
3	8	2
+ 4	5	9

Hundreds	Tens	Ones
4	0	4
+ 3	9	8

Hundreds	Tens	Ones
7	1	9
+ 1	4	3

Hundreds	Tens	Ones
5	5	6
+ 1	5	3

Hundreds	Tens	Ones
8	2	7
+ 1	4	4

Hundreds	Tens	Ones
6	3	4
+ 1	6	6

Hundreds	Tens	Ones
7	1	1
+ 2	1	9

Hundreds	Tens	Ones
3	8	9
+ 4	9	8

Solve the word problem and write the equation and the sum in the box.

Ari is practicing for a baking competition. She has baked 237 cookies and 486 cupcakes so far. How much food has she baked in all?

Hundreds	Tens	Ones
+		

213

Addition and Subtraction

Adding Three-Digit Numbers with Regrouping Using Place Value

You can use place value to help you add multi-digit numbers when you need to regroup.

Solve the equations below by using the place-value strategy and write the answers on the lines.

804 + 128 =

___ + ___ + ___

___ + ___ + ___

___ + ___ + ___ = ___

705 + 219 =

___ + ___ + ___

___ + ___ + ___

___ + ___ + ___ = ___

416 + 338 =

___ + ___ + ___

___ + ___ + ___

___ + ___ + ___ = ___

227 + 167 =

___ + ___ + ___

___ + ___ + ___

___ + ___ + ___ = ___

514 + 379 =

___ + ___ + ___

___ + ___ + ___

___ + ___ + ___ = ___

621 + 149 =

___ + ___ + ___

___ + ___ + ___

___ + ___ + ___ = ___

Solve the word problem by using the place-value strategy and write the equation and the sum on the lines.

Clarissa is also practicing for the baking competition. She has baked 207 pies and 486 muffins. How much food has she baked in all?

___ + ___ + ___

___ + ___ + ___

___ + ___ + ___ = ___

Addition and Subtraction

Subtracting Three-Digit Numbers by Regrouping

Subtracting hundreds, tens, and ones sometimes involves regrouping. If the top number in a column is less than the bottom number, you need to regroup by borrowing from the next highest place value.

Solve the equations by regrouping. Write the differences in the boxes below.

Hundreds	Tens	Ones
7	3	1
− 2	3	7

Hundreds	Tens	Ones
6	2	5
− 3	1	7

Hundreds	Tens	Ones
9	3	0
− 3	7	2

Hundreds	Tens	Ones
4	1	3
− 1	3	6

Hundreds	Tens	Ones
5	5	5
− 2	8	7

Hundreds	Tens	Ones
6	4	1
− 4	6	4

Hundreds	Tens	Ones
9	3	0
− 3	0	2

Hundreds	Tens	Ones
2	1	0
− 1	3	6

Hundreds	Tens	Ones
3	7	4
− 2	0	9

Solve the word problem and write the problem and the answer in the box.

Eliza is writing a 550-word essay for school. She has already written 317 words. How many words does she have left to write?

Hundreds	Tens	Ones
−		

Addition and Subtraction

Addition and Subtraction Word Problems

Read each word problem carefully and look for clues to help you decide if you should add or subtract. Numbers and words can be clues!

Circle the clues and use them to decide which operation and symbol you will use in your equation. Solve and write the answers on the lines below.

Lottie and Javier had to draw circles for an art project. Javier drew 138 circles. Lottie drew 214 more circles than Javier. How many circles did Lottie draw?

____ 〇 ____ = ____

Clare had 763 marbles. She gave 414 marbles to Eli. How many marbles does Clare have left?

____ 〇 ____ = ____

Eduardo and Mac both collect trading cards. Eduardo has 525 cards. Mac has 138 fewer cards than Eduardo. How many cards does Mac have?

____ 〇 ____ = ____

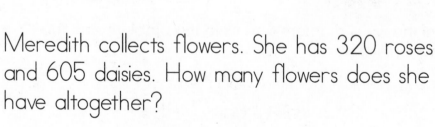

Meredith collects flowers. She has 320 roses and 605 daisies. How many flowers does she have altogether?

____ 〇 ____ = ____

Multiplication

Look at the groups in each of the illustrations below and use repeated addition to help you solve the multiplication equation.

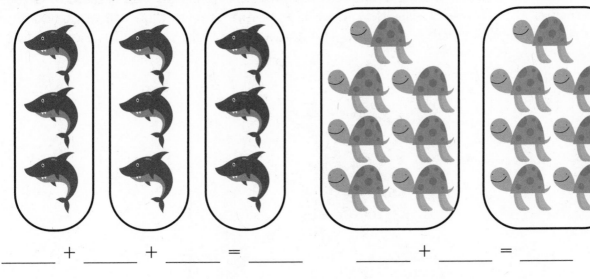

_____ + _____ + _____ = _____   _____ + _____ = _____

_____ X _____ = _____   _____ X _____ = _____

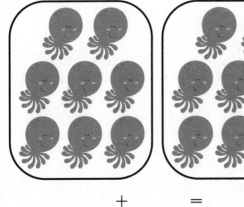   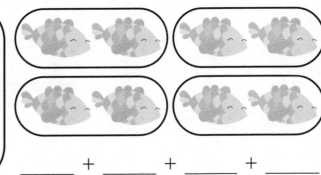

_____ + _____ + _____ + _____

= _____

_____ + _____ = _____   _____ X _____ = _____

_____ X _____ = _____

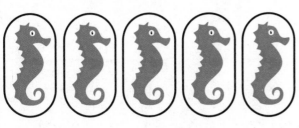

_____ + _____ + _____ +

_____ + _____ = _____   _____ + _____ + _____ = _____

_____ X _____ = _____   _____ X _____ = _____

217

Multiplication

Find Unknowns

A letter can be used in place of an unknown factor. When a letter is used, it is known as a variable because its value varies when used in different equations. Use the multiplication table on page 154 if you need help solving for the variable.

Example:
$$n \times 4 = 12$$

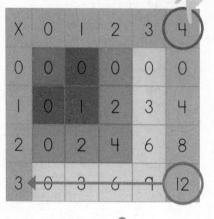

$$n = 3$$

$6 \times v = 36$	$6 \times \underline{\hspace{1cm}} = 36$

$6 \times v = 36$

$6 \times \underline{\hspace{1cm}} = 36$

$10 \times 4 = k$

$10 \times 4 = \underline{\hspace{1cm}}$

$a \times 7 = 35$

$\underline{\hspace{1cm}} \times 7 = 35$

$3 \times 9 = d$

$3 \times 9 = \underline{\hspace{1cm}}$

$4 \times t = 20$

$4 \times \underline{\hspace{1cm}} = 20$

$8 \times 0 = m$

$8 \times 0 = \underline{\hspace{1cm}}$

$i \times 8 = 64$

$\underline{\hspace{1cm}} \times 8 = 64$

$q \times 7 = 63$

$\underline{\hspace{1cm}} \times 7 = 63$

$6 \times u = 66$

$6 \times \underline{\hspace{1cm}} = 66$

$6 \times 12 = c$

$6 \times 12 = \underline{\hspace{1cm}}$

$n \times 2 = 18$

$\underline{\hspace{1cm}} \times 2 = 18$

$7 \times e = 49$

$7 \times \underline{\hspace{1cm}} = 49$

Division

Exploring Division

You can use an array to help you solve a division problem. In division, start with the whole set, known as the dividend. The divisor is one part of the dividend. The quotient is the answer (and the other part of the dividend). Use the arrays below to help solve the problems. Write the quotients on the lines below.

How many juice boxes are there altogether? _____

Place the juice boxes into groups of 5 by circling equal sets.

How many groups are there? _____

$25 \div 5 =$ _____

How many cupcakes are there altogether? _____

Place the cupcakes into groups of 4 by circling equal sets.

How many groups are there? _____

$24 \div 4 =$ _____

How many cookies are there altogether? _____

Place the cookies into groups of 10 by circling equal sets.

How many groups are there? _____

$30 \div 10 =$ _____

How many ice-cream cones are there altogether? _____

Place the ice-cream cones into groups of 8 by circling equal sets.

How many groups are there? _____

$24 \div 8 =$ _____

Fractions

Color the parts of the shapes to match the fractions.

$\frac{1}{2}$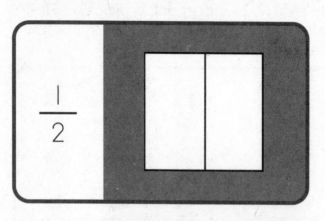

$\frac{2}{3}$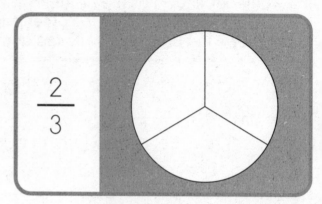

$\frac{7}{8}$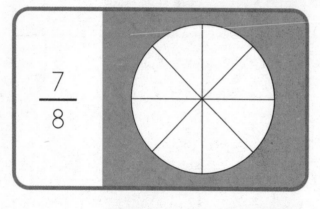

$\frac{1}{4}$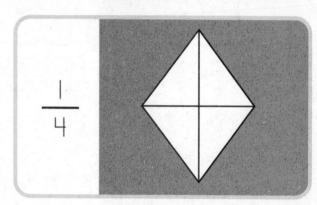

$\frac{4}{6}$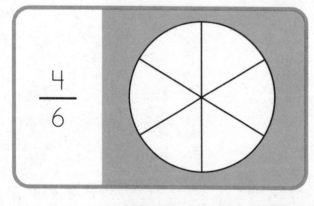

$\frac{5}{6}$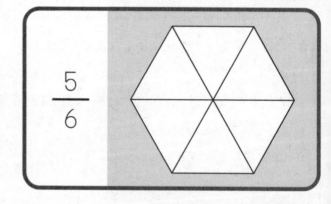

$\frac{1}{2}$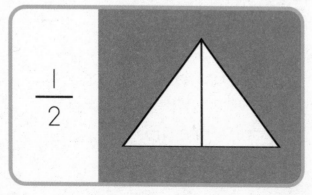

$\frac{4}{4}$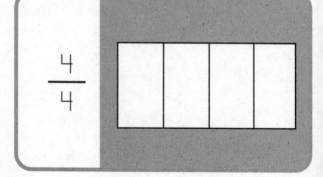

Break each number line below into equal parts based on each fraction's denominator. Write each fraction on the number line and then place a dot on the correct fraction. HINT: The denominator, or bottom number, tells you how many equal parts there will be in all.

$\frac{3}{8}$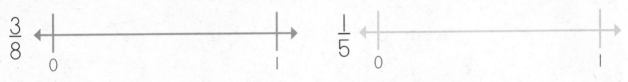

0   1

$\frac{1}{5}$

0   1

$\frac{2}{4}$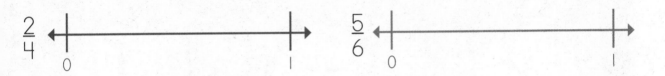

0   1

$\frac{5}{6}$

0   1

$\frac{4}{10}$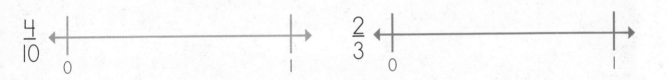

0   1

$\frac{2}{3}$

0   1

$\frac{6}{7}$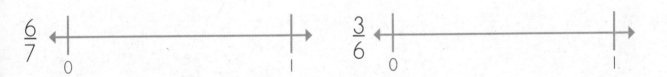

0   1

$\frac{3}{6}$

0   1

$\frac{2}{2}$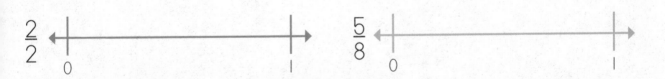

0   1

$\frac{5}{8}$

0   1

If a number line is partitioned into fifths, how many equal parts are there? _____

If a number line is partitioned into thirds, how many equal parts are there? _____

Time

What time is it? Write the time under each clock.

What time is it? Draw the hands on the clocks to match the digital times.

1:37

11:02

7:56

4:44

10:29

2:18

Data Management

Making a Scaled Bar Graph

Use the tally graph data to make a scaled bar graph. Then answer the questions. Write the answers on the lines below.

mystery	ⅣⅣ ⅣⅣ IIII
adventure	ⅣⅣ ⅣⅣ ⅣⅣ ⅣⅣ
fantasy	ⅣⅣ ⅣⅣ IIII
biographies	IIII
picture books	ⅣⅣ ⅣⅣ II

Types of Books

Number of Students	mystery	adventure	fantasy	biographies	picture books
22					
20					
18					
16					
14					
12					
10					
8					
6					
4					
2					

How many kids like fantasy books? _____

How many kids like picture books? _____

What kind of book is the most popular? _____

What kind of book is the least popular? _____

How many kids voted altogether? _____

Geometry

Write how many line segments each figure has on the lines below.

_____   _____   _____   _____   _____

Look at the figures below and write whether the figures are open or closed.

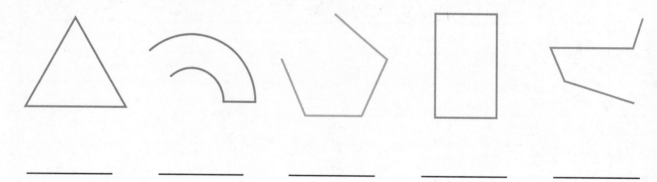

_____   _____   _____   _____   _____

Write how many sides each polygon has on the lines below. Then write the name of the polygons.

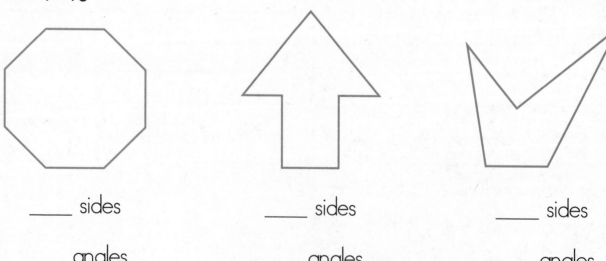

____ sides   ____ sides   ____ sides

____ angles   ____ angles   ____ angles

_____   _____   _____

ANSWER KEY

Page 7

Vocabulary

Syllables

A syllable is a word or part of a word that is heard when you make one clap.

Example:
1 syllable	2 syllables	3 syllables
bear	li/on	el/e/phant

Read the words below out loud as you clap each syllable. How many syllables do you hear? Sort the words into the correct categories based on the number of claps you hear. Write them on the lines below.

wolf pelican monkey snake kangaroo whale
porcupine turtle giraffe octopus walrus seal

1 SYLLABLE	2 SYLLABLES	3 SYLLABLES
wolf	monkey	pelican
snake	turtle	kangaroo
whale	giraffe	porcupine
seal	walrus	octopus

Page 8

Vocabulary

Decoding New Words

If you are not certain how to read a word, it may help you to figure out the word's syllables, or chunks. A helpful hint is to remember that there will usually be at least one vowel (A, E, I, O, U, and sometimes Y) in each syllable in a word.

Example: dif/ fer/ ent

Break these words into syllables based on the vowels in each chunk and write how many syllables each word has on the line across from each word. Use a colored pencil to show the division of the words.

h o l/i/d a y	3 syllables
s n o w/m a n	2 syllables
h a l l/w a y	2 syllables
g a r/d e n	2 syllables
t o/g e/t h e r	3 syllables
w i n/t e r	2 syllables
s k a/t i n g	2 syllables
e x/p e r/i/m e n t	4 syllables
e x/c i/t e d	3 syllables
s c i e n/t i s t	3 syllables

Page 11

Reading Comprehension

Following Directions

Follow the directions below to complete the neighborhood map.

1. Draw an American flag on a pole in front of the post office.
2. Draw your house in the southeast corner of the map.
3. Draw two children beside the school.
4. Draw a fire truck inside of the fire station.
5. Draw a car on Main Street driving toward the gas station.
6. Draw a librarian at the library holding a book.
7. Draw yourself on Orange Street near your house.

Page 14

Reading Comprehension

Sequencing

Sequencing is putting directions in the correct order.
You can sequence the order of any activity.

Read the steps for building a snowman below. Write the numbers in the boxes to put the steps in order and then rewrite the steps in the correct order on the lines below.

Give your snowman a hat and scarf	5
Roll one small, one medium, and one large snowball.	1
Put a stick on each side of the medium snowball for arms.	4
Place the small snowball on top of the medium snowball.	3
Put a mouth, button eyes, and a carrot nose on the small snowball.	6
Place the medium snowball on top of the large snowball.	2

1. Roll one small, one medium, and one large snowball.
2. Place the medium snowball on top of the large snowball.
3. Place the small snowball on top of the medium snowball.
4. Put a stick on each side of the medium snowball for arms.
5. Give your snowman a hat and scarf
6. Put a mouth, button eyes, and a carrot nose on the small snowball.

Page 15

Reading Comprehension

Sequencing

You can also sequence the order of a story that you read.
Read the passage below and find out what happened in the beginning, middle, and end of the story.

Gail's Girls

Gail has three little girls. They love to bake! They always help Gail make wonderful cakes and cupcakes at home. First, they help her take out all the ingredients. Then they help Gail mix the ingredients in a big bowl. They love to lick the spoon after mixing! After the cakes and cupcakes are finished, they all have a tea party in the backyard.

Answer the questions about the story. Write your answers on the lines below.

What did Gail's girls help her do?

They helped her make cakes and cupcakes.

What do they help her do first?

They help her take out all the ingredients.

What do they help her do next?

They help her mix the ingredients in a big bowl.

What do they love to do after mixing the ingredients?

They love to lick the spoon after mixing.

What do they do last?

They have a tea party in the backyard.

Page 16

Reading Comprehension

Compare and Contrast

When we compare and contrast things, we tell how they are alike and how they are different.

A great way to compare and contrast things is to use a Venn diagram.

A Venn diagram is made of two large overlapping circles. Each side of the circles tells how things are different. The middle tells how they are alike.

Think about what you know about elephants and giraffes. Write in the Venn diagram about how they are alike and how they are different.

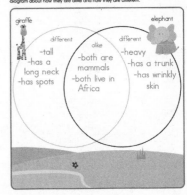

giraffe — different: -tall -has a long neck -has spots

alike: -both are mammals -both live in Africa

elephant — different: -heavy -has a trunk -has wrinkly skin

Page 17

Reading Comprehension

Compare and Contrast

Read the passage below and compare and contrast the characters in the story.

Maddy and Lucy Go Camping

Maddy and Lucy love to go camping. Every time their mom and dad tell them they are planning a trip to the lake, they squeal with delight. For Maddy, it means time to swim and read quietly under a tree. For Lucy, it means time for board games and water skiing. Maddy loves all the camping food. Her favorite foods are hot dogs and roasted marshmallows. Lucy likes to bring healthier food from home. She eats raw carrots and granola bars while they go camping. While Maddy and Lucy both love to go camping for different reasons, they are both sad to leave the lake every time one of their camping trips comes to an end.

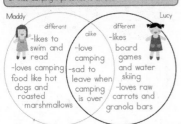

Maddy — different: -likes to swim and read -loves camping food like hot dogs and roasted marshmallows

alike: -love camping -sad to leave when camping is over

Lucy — different: -likes board games and water skiing -loves raw carrots and granola bars

Page 18

Reading Comprehension

Facts and Opinions

A fact is something that can be proven with evidence.
An opinion is something that is a personal belief.

Example: It is a fact that there are fifty states in the United States.
In my opinion, strawberry is the best flavor of ice cream.

Read each sentence below and determine if it is a fact or an opinion. Circle the correct answer.

Two nickels equal a dime.	**fact** opinion
Dogs are better pets than cats.	fact **opinion**
Chicago is a city in Illinois.	**fact** opinion
The American flag is red, white, and blue.	**fact** opinion
My mom makes the best chocolate-chip cookies.	fact **opinion**
Kids should be able to choose their own bedtime.	fact **opinion**
Four quarters equal one dollar.	**fact** opinion
Thanksgiving is everyone's favorite holiday.	fact **opinion**
A blue whale is the largest whale.	**fact** opinion
Everyone loves to go swimming.	fact **opinion**
It is fun to ride a roller coaster.	fact **opinion**
There are twelve months in a year.	**fact** opinion

Page 19

Reading Comprehension

Facts and Opinions

Facts can be proven by reading about the subject, looking it up online, or asking a parent or teacher. Opinions can mean that one person may believe something while another may disagree.

Read the sentences below and write the word fact or opinion beside each sentence.

Our family should have a dog.	opinion
The cafeteria should serve French fries every day.	opinion
Everyone loves to go camping.	opinion
Ten dimes equal one dollar.	fact
The city of Portland is in Oregon.	fact

Write two sentences that are facts.

Write two sentences that are your opinions.

Page 20

Reading Comprehension

Main Idea
The main idea is what the story is mainly about.

Example: A book titled *Tammy's First Bus Ride* is probably about a bus ride. That is the main idea.

Read the passage.

> Anthony and Rebecca love to travel. They have flown to many different countries around the world and have loved every one of them. Their favorite country to visit was Spain, but they also loved France and Japan.

Circle the main idea.
- Anthony and Rebecca's favorite country is Spain.
- Anthony and Rebecca have traveled to France.
- (Anthony and Rebecca enjoy traveling around the world.)

> Barry and Marion rode their bikes to the grocery store. They bought all of their favorite candy and snacks. Barry likes chocolate, and Marion likes pretzels. They decided to share their treats. Marion discovered that she likes chocolate, and Barry found out that he likes pretzels!

Circle the main idea.
- Marion likes pretzels.
- Barry and Marion rode their bikes to the grocery store.
- (Barry and Marion tried new snacks and liked them.)

Page 21

Reading Comprehension

Main Idea and Supporting Details
Look for the main idea and supporting details as you read the passage below.

> **Earth Day**
> Today is Earth Day! Our class is learning about recycling. Recycling means taking something that has been thrown away and making something new out of it. Recycling is good for the planet because recycling and reusing things means we are throwing away less garbage. We are reusing bottles in class today by making planters out of the used water bottles. I chose a yellow flower to put in my new planter. I like Earth Day.

What is the main idea of this passage?
The importance of recycling.

What are some of the supporting details in the passage?
Recycling is good for the planet.
There are a number of ways to recycle.

What was made from the recycled water bottles?
planters

Page 22

Reading Comprehension

Making Predictions
Making a prediction means thinking about what you are reading and making a guess about what might happen next. Clues in the text and things you already know can help you predict what might happen next.

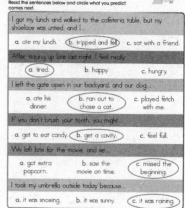

Read the sentences below and circle what you predict comes next.

I got my lunch and walked to the cafeteria table, but my shoelace was untied, and I...
a. ate my lunch. (b. tripped and fell) c. sat with a friend.

After staying up late last night, I feel really...
(a. tired.) b. happy. c. hungry.

I left the gate open in our backyard, and our dog...
a. ate his dinner. (b. ran out to chase a cat.) c. played fetch with me.

If you don't brush your teeth, you might...
a. get to eat candy. (b. get a cavity.) c. feel full.

We left late for the movie, and we...
a. got extra popcorn. b. saw the movie on time. (c. missed the beginning.)

I took my umbrella outside today because...
a. it was snowing. b. it was sunny. (c. it was raining.)

Page 24

Reading Comprehension

Fiction
Some stories are realistic fiction, which means even though the story is made up, it could happen in real life.

There are also fairy tales, which often have imaginary characters like wizards and dragons.

Fiction stories can also be fables, which are fictional stories with a lesson or moral. Fables often have animals as the main characters.

Read the passage below and circle what kind of fiction it is.

The Little Red Hen
The little red hen was a very hard worker. She cleaned the farm, cooked the food, and took care of her chicks. One day, she found a grain of wheat. "Who will help me plant this wheat?" she asked.

"Not I," replied the dog, duck, cat, and pig.

So she planted it herself.

After the seed grew and the wheat was harvested and ground into flour, the little red hen asked, "Who will help me bake the bread?"

"Not I," replied the dog, duck, cat, and pig.

So she baked the bread herself.

When the bread was baked, she and her chicks began to eat.

"May we have some bread?" asked the dog, duck, cat, and pig.

"No, you may not!" said the little red hen. "I did all the work myself! My chicks and I will eat the bread."

From then on, the dog, duck, cat, and pig tried to be more helpful to the little red hen and their other friends.

a. realistic fiction
b. fairy tale
(c. fable)

Page 25

Reading Comprehension

Fiction
Look at the book titles below and draw a line to the correct type of fiction.

realistic fiction

fable

fairy tale

Page 26

Reading Comprehension

Nonfiction
Nonfiction reading can explain, inform, and persuade. The nonfiction information shared must be based on factual information, which means the information can be proven to be true.

Biographies are true stories about a real person's life.

Informational text provide facts about people, places, things, and events. Sometimes this type of nonfiction text will give information about a person's job, such as a farmer or doctor.

When someone writes a letter and shares true information, it is nonfiction text.

Read the passage below and answer the question.

> Dear Nana,
> I miss you a lot! I wish I could come visit you, but right now I have to stay home because it is not our family vacation time.
> What have you been doing to stay busy? I have been doing a lot of things! Two of my favorites are learning to ride a horse and playing board games.
> The horse I am riding is named Blaze because he has a white streak on his forehead. He is very gentle to ride. I love when he gallops!
> I have been playing a lot of board games almost every day. My favorite games are word games. I love trying to spell words I know and I have even learned a few new ones. Maybe we can play some games when I finally get to visit you!
> Love,
> Eila

What is some true information that Eila shared with her grandmother in her letter?

Eila has been playing a lot of board games.

Page 27

Reading Comprehension

Nonfiction
Look at the book titles below and draw a line to the correct type of nonfiction.

informational text

biography

Page 31

Text Features

Table of Contents
The table of contents tells you what information can be found in a book and what page it begins on.

Read the table of contents below.

Use the table of contents above to help you answer the questions. Write your answers on the lines below.

How many chapters are in the book?
Four

What chapter can be found on page 10?
Chapter 3: Dolphin Babies

If you think dolphins are found around the world, what chapter will help you find out if that is true?
Chapter 2: Where Dolphins Live

To find out what dolphins eat, what page would you turn to?
2

Page 32

Text Features

Index
The index is at the end of the book. Some books have them, and others don't. It is a list of all the topics that are in the book and all the pages where the topics are located. The words or phrases listed in the index are in alphabetical order.

Read the index below.

Use the index above to help you answer the questions. Write your answers on the lines below.

On what pages can you find information about dolphins' habitats?
4–5

On what pages can you find information about dolphin food?
2, 3, and 9

What topic can be found on pages 8, 10, and 11?
Predators

If you wanted to find out about dolphin babies, what page or pages should you turn to?
6 and 7

Page 33

Text Features

Glossary

Some books have a list of words on a certain page or in the back of the book called a glossary. A glossary is like a little dictionary. It gives the meanings of important words from the book. The words in the glossary are in alphabetical order.

Take a look at the glossary below and find the information needed to answer the questions.

GLOSSARY

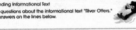

Blowhole	The hole on top of a dolphin's head that it uses to breathe air
Intelligent	The ability to think deeply
Mammal	A warm-blooded animal that breathes air and typically has live babies
Pod	A group of dolphins that lives and travels together
Predator	An animal that eats other animals for food

What is a group of dolphins called?

A pod

What does the word "mammal" mean?

A warm-blooded animal that breathes air and typically has live babies

What does a dolphin use its blowhole for?

It helps them breathe air.

Page 34

Text Features

Diagrams

Diagrams often provide details beyond the textual information shared in nonfiction text.

Read this paragraph and study the diagram.

Cone-shaped volcanos are the most common type of volcano. A volcano may erupt from its crater or from a secondary vent. The side of a cone-shaped volcano is called the flank. Layers of ash and lava build up on the flank over time due to multiple eruptions. The more eruptions there are, the bigger the mountain will become. When magma travels upward and comes out of this crater, it is called lava.

Answer the questions on the lines below. Check the box to share where you found the answer to each question.

What is the area called where a secondary vent reaches the surface of a volcano?

Secondary cone.

Did you answer this question by ☐ reading the text? ☑ studying the diagram?

Why does a volcano's flank get bigger over time?

Layers of ash and lava build up over time due to multiple eruptions.

Did you answer this question by ☑ reading the text? ☐ studying the diagram?

What falls from an ash cloud?

Ash

Did you answer this question by ☐ reading the text? ☑ studying the diagram?

Page 37

Nonfiction Text

Comprehending Informational Text

Answer the questions about the informational text "An Amazing Animal." Write your answers on the lines below.

What are four facts you learned about octopuses?

_____

What can an octopus do if it needs to get away quickly?

An octopus can get away by shooting out a jet of water and zooming away backward.

What is the name of the biggest species of octopus?

Giant Pacific octopus

What is the name of the smallest species of octopus?

Star-sucker pygmy octopus

Page 39

Nonfiction Text

Comprehending Informational Text

Answer the questions about the informational text "River Otters." Write your answers on the lines below.

What are three facts you learned about river otters?

_____

What do you know about otters' dens?

Female and male river otters live in different parts of the den.

What is a group of swimming river otters called?

A raft

How are river otters playful?

They like to slide down slippery hills on their bellies, belly flop into the water, and play fight with their friends.

Page 41

Nonfiction Text

Comprehending Biographies

Answer the questions about the biography "Terry Fox." Write your answers on the lines below.

What are three facts you learned about Terry Fox?

_____

What gave Terry the idea to run his Marathon of Hope?

Terry wanted to help encourage other cancer patients.

What did the doctors have to do to save Terry's life?

The doctors had to perform surgery to remove most of Terry's right leg.

How many years passed between Terry's news that he had cancer to when he ran his Marathon of Hope?

4 years

Page 43

Nonfiction Text

Comprehending Persuasive Text

Answer the questions about the persuasive letter Marcia wrote her parents. Write your answers on the lines below in complete sentences.

What does Marcia want to be given for her tenth birthday?

A cell phone

Marcia gave her opinion for why she thinks she should get a cell phone for her birthday. What are two of her reasons? Be sure to include her supporting details in your answer.

A cell phone would help Marcia stay in contact with her parents through text messages and allow her to take photos of special memories in their family life.

What do you think Marcia's mom and dad will decide to do? Why do you think that?

_____

Page 45

Fictional Text

Comprehending Realistic Fiction

Answer the questions about the realistic fiction passage "Josh's Super Sandwich." Write your answers on the lines below using complete sentences.

What are two things Josh did before making his super sandwich?

He took a shower and took the ingredients he needed out of the refrigerator.

Why do you think Josh called his sandwich a "supersonic, triple-decker" sandwich? Support your reasoning using text from the passage.

_____

If you could create a super sandwich, what ingredients would you use?

_____

Draw a picture of your super sandwich below. Be sure to label each of its layers!

Page 47

Fictional Text

Comprehending Fictional Text

Answer the questions about the fiction passage "Claire the Clumsy Cow." Write your answers in complete sentences.

Why was Claire called Claire the Clumsy Cow?

Because Claire is always tripping over things and falling down.

What was the problem that led to Claire falling into the stream?

Claire leaned forward to take a drink of water from the stream and slipped.

What did Claire say that let you know she enjoyed the water?

"I am enjoying floating in this stream."

What does Claire mean when she called herself a "buoyant bovine"? Use text from the passage to support your reasoning

She means she is a cow that can float.

Did you make a personal connection to this passage? Think of a time when you were clumsy like Claire.

_____

Page 51

Fictional Text

Comprehending a Greek Myth

Answer the questions about the Greek myth "Midas and His Golden Touch." Write your answers in complete sentences on the lines below. Be sure you use text from the story to aid in answering the questions.

Who are the three characters in this story?

King Midas, Marigold, and the stranger.

What are the five settings for this story?

The treasury room, the king's bedroom, the dining room, the rose garden, and the river.

Page 52

Fictional Text

Analyzing a Greek Myth

You were asked to think about what parents were trying to teach their children when reading the "Midas and His Golden Touch" myth. Which moral best matches the myth? Check one of the four boxes below and then use text from the myth to justify the reasoning for your choice on the lines. Write your response using complete sentences.

- [ ] It is important to be kind to everyone because then others will be kind to you.
- [x] Do not be greedy because it can cause problems in your life.
- [ ] Always be honest because people will believe you if you are wrongly blamed.
- [ ] Listen to the advice of older people because their wisdom can help you make good decisions.

Page 53

Fictional Text

Analyzing a Greek Myth

If you think about who is telling a story, such as a myth, when you are reading it, then you are trying to figure out who is the narrator. The narrator can be a character in the story or can be a voice who is not a character in the story, but can explain to readers what is happening and how characters are thinking and feeling.

Who is the narrator of this story? Check one of the four boxes and then use text from the myth to justify the reasoning for your choice on the lines below.

- [ ] King Midas
- [x] A Narrator Voice
- [ ] Marigold
- [ ] Stranger

Draw an illustration of what the stranger looked like in your mind when you were reading the myth. Then list the words, phrases, and/or sentences that inspired your stranger drawing.

Page 55

Fictional Text

Comprehending Fables

Answer the questions about the fable "The Lion and the Mouse." Write your answers on the lines in complete sentences.

Which moral best matches the table? Check one box and then write your reasoning on the lines below.

- [ ] Never, ever give up.
- [x] Do to others as you want them to do to you.
- [ ] There is always a way to figure something out.

What word do you think best describes Mouse's personality? What actions and dialogue in the fable support your reasoning?

Page 57

Opinion Text

Comprehending Opinion Text

Answer the questions about the opinion passage "The Cleanup Crew." Write your answers on the lines below in complete sentences.

What is the author's opinion on cleaning up after dinner?

It takes too long when you clean up alone.

What are the details for doing the table cleaning chore?

You have to put away the food, carry the dishes to the sink, wrap up the leftovers, and wipe down the tabletop and counters.

What are the details for completing the floor and dog bowl cleaning chore?

You have to sweep the floor under the table and around the counters and then use a dust pan to pick up the crumbs. You also have to put fresh water in the dog bowl.

Which of the two chores would you prefer to do and why?

Page 59

Opinion Text

Comprehending Opinion Text

Answer the questions about the opinion passage "Chocolate or Regular Milk?" Write your answers on the lines below in complete sentences.

How did the author make sure his milk-tasting test would be fair?

The author poured the same amount of milk into the glasses and ate the same sandwich with both. The author also wore a blindfold.

What does the author like about chocolate milk? Look for supporting details in the table to help you answer the question.

The author likes the taste, texture, and the flavor with the sandwich.

Look at the table in the passage. In which category did the author like regular milk the same as chocolate milk?

The flavor with the sandwich.

What is your opinion on regular milk versus chocolate milk? Do not forget to include details in your answer to support your reasoning.

Page 61

Letters

Comprehending a Letter

Answer the questions about the letter Andy wrote to his parents. Write your answers on the lines below.

Where was Andy when he wrote the letter?

Andy was at summer camp.

Write two things Andy told his parents about camp life.

Andy attended a campfire sing-along and had a delicious pancake breakfast.

Why do you believe Andy's opinion of camp changed?

Who are three people you would like to write a letter to, and why?

Page 64

Posters

Reading and Comprehending Posters

Just like a story, when a poster is made, the author has designed it for a purpose.

Authors sometimes design posters to provide information.

Authors also design posters to make the information easy to read and understand. Posters often have big, bold print and illustrations.

Look at the posters below. What is the message or information the author wants you to know? Write your answers on the lines below.

LOST DOG

What does the author want the reader to know?

They lost their dog.

What is the important information on this poster?

The description of Spot and the contact information.

BABYSITTER FOR HIRE!

What does the author want the reader to know?

She is looking for a babysitting job.

What is the important information on this poster?

Her qualifications and contact information.

Page 80

Practicing Cursive Writing

Print and Cursive

Draw a line to match the print letters to the cursive letters. Then trace the cursive letters.

A B C D E F G H I J K L M

N O P Q R S T U V W X Y Z

Page 82

ABC Order

ABC Order

Putting words into ABC order means they are in the order of the alphabet. If there are multiple words with the same first letter, you need to look at the second letter and sometimes the third letter to put the words in the correct alphabetical order.

Example: diamond   dog   doughnut

Diamond is the first word in ABC order because i comes before o in the alphabet. The remaining two words both have an o after the first letter. Dog is the next word in ABC order because g comes before u in the alphabet. The last word in ABC order is doughnut.

Put all the words in ABC order. Then rewrite them all in order on the lines below.

pole · shell · tusks · sea star · table · apple · pond · apron · turtle · shark · astronaut · porcupine

apple
apron
astronaut
pole
pond
porcupine
sea star
shark
shell
table
turtle
tusks

Titles

Capital Letters for Titles
Movie titles, book titles, and titles of plays or poems are written using a capital letter for almost every word in the title. Only the small words, such as the, to, in, if, and, or, and on are not capitalized, unless one of those words comes at the beginning or end of the title.
Example: Humpty Dumpty
            Aladdin and the Magic Lamp
Look at the three movie posters below. Write the title next to each movie poster using correct capitalization.
Coming Soon:

 Twinkle, Twinkle, Little Star

 The Little Mermaid

 Cluck, Cluck, Moo

Write your own book title on the lines below. Be sure to capitalize it properly.

Grammar

Homophones
Homophones are words that have the same pronunciation but different spellings and different meanings.
Example: sun and son
Look at the pictures below and circle the correct homophone word.

see (sea)	ate (eight)	(bear) bare
flour (flower)	be (bee)	(deer) dear

Each sentence below has a word in it that is the wrong homophone. Circle the incorrect homophone and write the correct one on the line after the sentence.

I bought a new (pear) of shoes today! __pair__
(Eye) am going skating at the rink tonight. __I__
Let (right) a letter to a friend. __write__
I can't (weight) for my birthday party next week. __wait__
Did you (sea) that shooting star in the sky? __see__
I'm going to pick some (flours) for my mom. __flowers__

Grammar

Homographs
Homographs are words that have the same spelling, but different pronunciations and different meanings.
Example: bass and bass
Look at the two pictures in each box below. Write the correct homograph to complete the two sentences in each box.

I like the pretty **bow** in your hair	A **bow** can be a sign of respect.
The **wind** is blowing very hard!	My brother will **wind** up the toy.
A **dove** landed on my windowsill!	Jason **dove** into the cold water.

Grammar

Homonyms
Homonyms are words that have the same pronunciation and the same spelling but have different meanings.
Example: right and right
Look at the two pictures in each box below. Write the correct homograph to complete the two sentences in each box.

I wrote a **letter** to my best friend.	"I" is a word and a **letter** of the alphabet.
A **palm** tree can grow very tall.	I have ten cents in my **palm**.
My dad will **park** our car.	I love to play at the **park**.

Grammar

Concrete Nouns Versus Abstract Nouns
Concrete nouns represent people, places, things, or objects that can be seen, heard, touched, tasted, or smelled.
Abstract nouns represent ideas, concepts, or feelings. An idea, concept, or feeling cannot be seen, heard, touched, tasted, or smelled.
Example: Eagle
         Eagle is a concrete noun. You can see the eagle.
         Freedom
         Freedom is an abstract noun. You cannot see freedom, but you can picture something in your mind that represents freedom.
Read each sentence below. Write the sentence's concrete noun in the first column and the abstract noun in the second column.

Sentences	Concrete Nouns	Abstract Nouns
1. The older man enjoyed talking about his childhood.	man	childhood
2. My mom shows her love by giving me a hug.	mom	love
3. The lion was experiencing loneliness at the zoo.	lion	loneliness
4. The bird rested in peace on the branch.	bird	peace
5. Tisha found happiness in doing things for others.	Tisha	happiness
6. The knight was known for his bravery.	knight	bravery
7. Danny thinks getting an education is important.	Danny	education

---

Grammar

Comparative Adverbs
Comparative adverbs are used when comparing two of something.
A comparative adverb may be a:
 • single word
 • one-syllable adverb with -er suffix
 • phrase
Example: A sundae tastes better than a popsicle. A cheetah is faster than a lion. Dominic paints less carefully than Randall.

worse	more cheaply	longer	as slowly as
less	more seriously	later	as quickly as

Read each sentence below. Use the comparative adverbs in the table above to complete the sentences.
1. The box is __longer__ than it is tall.
2. Did William finish the race __as quickly as__ his brother?
3. Getting sick is __worse__ than getting a shot.
4. The movie starts __later__ than the game.
5. Candice took the dance contest __more seriously__ than Joseph.
6. The soup did not boil __as slowly as__ the stew.
7. The shirt fabric was made __more cheaply__ than the coat fabric.
8. The remote control car costs __less__ than the bicycle.

Grammar

Superlative Adjectives
Superlative adjectives are used when comparing three or more nouns. Superlative adjectives are also used when comparing one thing to a group.
Example: Jupiter is the biggest planet in the solar system.
           That was the best movie ever made!

fastest	most happy	least important	worst
deepest	most famous	least sweet	best

Read each sentence below. Use the superlative adjectives in the table above to complete the sentences.
1. The furry dog was the __most happy__ when we came into the room.
2. What is the __deepest__ ocean in the world?
3. I think chocolate is the __best__ flavor of ice cream!
4. I think the __worst__ chore is having to take out smelly garbage!
5. What pitcher has thrown the __fastest__ pitch ever?
6. This pie is the __least sweet__ of all the pies we have tasted.
7. The __most famous__ movie cowboy was Roy Rogers.
8. The __least important__ ingredient in the recipe is the optional cheese topping.

Word Relationships

Literal Versus Nonliteral Meanings
Literal meaning means that every word in a sentence conveys exactly what is being said.
Non-literal meaning means that some of the words or a phrase in a sentence conveys something different than what is being said. Idioms are phrases that convey non-literal meanings.
Example: Cassandra is about to perform her magic act. Mom whispers, "Break a leg," to Cassandra before she goes on stage.

Do you think Cassandra's mom really wants her to break her leg? Of course she doesn't! This is an idiom that means "good luck." You probably have heard idioms before but may have never known that this is what these non-literal phrases are called.
Read the sentences in the left column and underline the idiom (non-literal meaning) in each sentence. In the right column, write what you think the literal meaning is that is being conveyed by the idiom.

Sentences with Idioms	Literal Meaning of Idioms
1. I have butterflies in my stomach because I know the Tilt-a-Whirl will have lots of twists and turns!	This person is nervous about going on a scary ride.
2. Cleaning my room will be a piece of cake because I keep it neat all of the time.	Cleaning the room will be easy because it is already neat.
3. Mr. Andersen looks at the time and says, "It is five o'clock. I will call it a day."	Mr. Andersen is done working for the day.
4. "Hang in there!" Brandy shouts to Marcus as he continues to run in the marathon.	Brandy is encouraging his friend as he runs.
5. Sara, the babysitter, says, "I think Trevor looks a bit under the weather," to Trevor's mother.	Sara thinks Trevor is feeling sick.

Word Relationships

Word Meaning Nuances
Nuance means a slightly different meaning about the same topic or idea. Words can be grouped based on a topic or idea from the least to the greatest intensity based on each word's meaning.
Example: When you think about describing someone "trying to get someone else's attention," the word meaning nuances from least to greatest could be:

Least	Greater	Still Greater	Greatest
whisper	call	holler	scream

Order each word set below from least to greatest intensity for each topic below.
Topic: move from one place to another
Word Set: run, stroll, walk, jog

Least	Greater	Still Greater	Greatest
stroll	walk	jog	run

Topic: reaction to a birthday party
Word Set: exciting, pleasant, nice, amazing

Least	Greater	Still Greater	Greatest
nice	pleasant	exciting	amazing

Topic: how someone might feel at the end of a long day at school
Word Set: exhausted, fatigued, tired, worn-out

Least	Greater	Still Greater	Greatest
worn-out	fatigued	tired	exhausted

Topic: motion of an object moving from one person to another
Word Set: hurl, toss, throw, fling

Least	Greater	Still Greater	Greatest
toss	throw	fling	hurl

Writing Sentences

Simple and Compound Sentences

A simple sentence is a sentence with only one clause. A clause is part of a sentence that has a subject (noun or pronoun) and a predicate (verb or verb phrase) in it.

A compound sentence is a sentence with two or more independent clauses.

An independent clause is a clause that has a subject and predicate and forms a complete thought. The two independent clauses are often joined together by a comma and a conjunction (e.g., but, so, for, and). If the conjunction because is used in a compound sentence, there will not be a comma placed before it.

Example: Simple: I saw a pretty bird in the pine tree.

Compound: I saw a pretty bird in the pine tree, but it was not as beautiful as the bird I saw in the tree yesterday.

Read the sentences in the left column. Write simple or compound in the middle column and your reasoning in the right column.

Sentences	Sentence Type	Explain Why
1. Everyone loves to watch Willy play ball, for he can throw a strong pitch.	compound	The sentence has two independent clauses.
2. Jamie ran out of money because she bought too much candy at the store.	compound	The sentence has two independent clauses.
3. The last time I went to the mall I enjoyed playing a lot of video games.	simple	The sentence only has one clause.
4. Everyone was busy, so I rode my bike to the park and played alone.	compound	The sentence has two independent clauses.
5. For our celebration dinner, we ate tamales, tostadas, beans, rice, and corn pudding.	simple	The sentence only has one clause.

Writing Sentences

Writing Complex Sentences

For each sentence below:
- circle the independent clause in red
- circle the dependent clause in blue
- put a box around the subordinating conjunction in purple

Even though my friend invited me to the game, I do not not want to go.

I held on to the swing because I felt dizzy.

She giggled loudly as the limber monkey did a somersault.

The dog jumped up high, so I gave him a tasty treat.

When you are wide awake in the morning, do a crossword puzzle.

Writing Sentences

Using Commas and Quotation Marks

Quotation marks go around all of the words that people or characters are saying.

Example: "Come over to my house," said Grace.
"Ok," said Ella, "but I can't stay very long."

Commas are used to separate what the person or character is saying from what the narrator is conveying.

Example: "Come over to my house," said Grace.
"Ok," said Ella, "but I can't stay very long."

Read the sentences below. Put quotation marks around what the people or characters are saying. Then add a comma to separate what the narrator is conveying from what the person or character is saying.

"I'm hungry," said Jacob.
Aaron said, "Let's go for a swim."
Sammy asked, "When will we get to the beach?"
"We are almost there," replied Lucas.
Stacey asked, "What time is it?"
Oscar said, "This is my favorite song!"

Sometimes quotation marks go around titles of short stories, songs, poems, and chapters.

Example: My favorite song is "Twinkle, Twinkle, Little Star."

Read the sentences below. Put the quotation marks where they are needed.

I read a lovely poem called "My Hungry Heart."
My favorite story is "The Princess and the Pea."
I can't get the "Chicken Dance" song out of my head!
I read chapter eight in "The Big Adventure" last night.
Have you ever read "The Tortoise and the Hare?"
"If You're Happy and You Know It" is my favorite song.

Writing Sentences

Now it is your turn. Read the sentences in the blue box below. Rewrite the sentences using the dialogue rules. Hint: There will be four paragraphs.

Mindy's mother came into the kitchen and tied the apron strings around her daughter's waist. Mindy, I think you're old enough to make our dinner rolls now. Really, Momma? squealed Mindy. I will be right here to help you, encouraged her mother. if you get stuck and are not sure what to do. Thank you, Momma! What is the first thing I need to do? inquired Mindy.

Mindy's mother came into the kitchen and tied the apron strings around her daughter's waist. "Mindy, I think you're old enough to make our dinner rolls now."

"Really, Momma?" squealed Mindy.

"I will be right here to help you," encouraged her mother, "if you get stuck and are not sure what to do."

"Thank you, Momma! What is the first thing I need to do?" inquired Mindy.

The Writing Process

Revising and Editing Writing

Read the passage. Use the checklist and proofreading marks to help Liberty revise and edit her draft. Then draw a picture to match the passage below.

Why Liberty Loves Independence Day

My name is liberty becauz my parents met at the statue of liberty in new york city, New York. july 4th is independence day, and it is my favorite holiday! My whole family had fun together all day and night this year. We went to the park wear we herd a band play patriotic songs, including america the beautiful. There were lots of families there and lots of activities, like a balloon toss. My sister and I were in a three-legged race, but we fell down and didn't win. Then we had a piknik dinner and ice cream for dessert. When it got dark, there was a fireworks show. That was the best part. There was even a special display of the Liberty Statue in bright lights, so my sister said I was in the show.

Writing a Fable

During the awards ceremony, Fox announces, "Ladies and gentlemen, Hare and Tortoise had a race within a race today to see who runs the fastest, and Tortoise won by a hair!" Everyone cheers, and Tortoise is then awarded a special trophy by Fox.

"Thank you, Fox, for my special award," Tortoise says from the heart, "and thank you, Hare, for running a race with me. Now let's go and nibble on some tasty lettuce together."

What do you think is the moral, or lesson, of the fable?

Put a check in one of the two boxes and explain why you chose that moral or lesson using phrases from the fable.

☑ Slow and steady wins the race.

☐ Small friends may prove to be great friends.

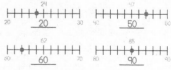

Number Sense

Least to Greatest

Put the numbers in order from least to greatest. Write the numbers on the lines below.

Example: 1,245 1,552 1,876 3,281

2,432	1,567	3,253	7,119	1,567 2,432 3,253 7,119
6,547	1,734	5,087	2,891	1,734 2,891 5,087 6,547
2,322	1,845	4,137	7,678	1,845 2,322 4,137 7,678
4,688	4,156	3,273	5,449	3,273 4,156 4,688 5,449
9,555	5,381	1,291	8,762	1,291 5,381 8,762 9,555

Number Hunt

Find the numbers that match the descriptions. Write the numbers on the lines below.

2,625   4,275   1,439
7,443   6,217   5,000

The number between 2,000 and 3,000 is	2,625
The number that has 0 tens and 0 ones is	5,000
The number between 1,000 and 1,500 is	1,439
The number between 4,000 and 5,000 is	4,275
The number that has 7 ones is	6,217
The number greater than all the others numbers is	7,443

Number Sense

Thousands, Hundreds, Tens, and Ones

Example:

Thousands   Hundreds   Tens   Ones

1 thousand + 1 hundred + 1 ten + 4 ones
= 1,114

Use the models below to count and write how many thousands, hundreds, tens, and ones there are on the lines below.

4 thousands + 2 hundreds + 7 tens + 9 ones
= 4,279

1 thousand + 4 hundreds + 1 ten + 4 ones
= 1,414

3 thousands + 3 hundreds + 1 ten + 1 one
= 3,311

2 thousands + 3 hundreds + 8 tens + 6 ones
= 2,386

Number Sense

Rounding to the Nearest Ten

Sometimes we use rounding to make an estimate to tell about how much a number is. When you round, you take the number to the nearest ten, hundred, or thousand, etc. Take a look at the number line to see how you can use it to help you understand rounding.

Place 56 on the number line.

Which tens is 56 between?

50 ——— 56 ——— 60

56 is between 50 and 60

Is 56 closer to 50 or closer to 60?

50 ——— 56 ——— 60

56 is closer to 60 than it is to 50.
So 56 rounds to 60

HINT: If the number in the ones place is equal to or greater than 5, round up to the next ten. If the number is less than 5, round down.

Use the number line to help you round. Read the numbers and mark them on the number lines with a dot. Then round to the nearest ten and write your answers on the lines below.

24
20 —— 20 —— 30

47
40 —— 50 —— 60

62
60 —— 60 —— 70

85
80 —— 90 —— 90

Round to the nearest ten. Write the answers on the lines.

57 __60__   34 __30__   82 __80__   75 __80__

Page 143

Rounding to the Nearest Hundred

You can use what you learned from rounding to the nearest ten to help you round to the nearest hundred. Use the number line to help you know when to round up or round down. Remember, rounding is used to make an estimate.

Place 372 on the number line.

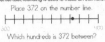

Which hundreds is 372 between?

To round, ask yourself if 372 is closer to 300 or 400. It is closer to 400, so 372 rounds to 400. You can also look at the number in the tens place. If the number is equal to or greater than 50, you will round up. 372 has 70 in the tens place, which is greater than 50, so it needs to be rounded up to 400.

Use the number line to help you round. Read the numbers and mark them on the number line with a dot. Then round to the nearest hundred and write your answers on the lines below.

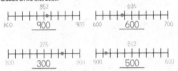

852 → **900**   636 → **600**

276 → **300**   512 → **500**

Round to the nearest hundred. Write the answers on the lines below.

467 **500**   298 **300**   553 **600**   725 **700**

The baby giraffe weighs 341 pounds. What is its weight rounded to the nearest hundred pounds? **300** pounds

Page 144

Expanded Notation

You can show numbers in expanded form in two different ways. Numbers can be written in words or written to show their separate place values.

Example: 4,393 = 4000 + 300 + 90 + 3
4,393 = four thousand + three hundred + ninety + three

Write the numbers in expanded form using place value numbers on the lines below.

3,596 = **3000** + **500** + **90** + **6**
2,185 = **2000** + **100** + **80** + **5**
4,526 = **4000** + **500** + **20** + **6**
1,732 = **1000** + **700** + **30** + **2**
4,444 = **4000** + **400** + **40** + **4**

Write the numbers in expanded form using words on the lines below.

5,276 = **five** thousands + **two** hundreds + **seven** tens + **six** ones
3,121 = **three** thousands + **one** hundreds + **two** tens + **one** ones
2,349 = **two** thousands + **three** hundreds + **four** tens + **nine** ones
1,587 = **one** thousands + **five** hundreds + **eight** tens + **seven** ones
1,995 = **one** thousands + **nine** hundreds + **nine** tens + **five** ones

Page 145

Adding and Subtracting Three-Digit Numbers

Practice adding and subtracting three-digit numbers. Write the answers in the boxes below.

Hundreds	Tens	Ones
3	2	1
+ 4	3	7
7	5	8

Hundreds	Tens	Ones
4	2	6
− 3	1	3
1	1	3

Hundreds	Tens	Ones
7	0	3
+ 1	1	3
8	1	6

Hundreds	Tens	Ones
7	1	4
− 5	1	3
2	0	1

Hundreds	Tens	Ones
2	9	9
− 1	0	7
1	9	2

Hundreds	Tens	Ones
4	6	2
+ 3	1	6
7	7	8

Hundreds	Tens	Ones
6	3	7
− 5	2	2
1	1	5

Hundreds	Tens	Ones
4	3	6
+ 2	6	2
6	9	8

Hundreds	Tens	Ones
5	5	3
− 4	3	2
1	2	1

Answer the number sense questions and write your answers on the lines.

What number is in the tens place of the number 2749? **7**
What number is in the ones place of the number 680? **0**
What number is in the hundreds place of the number 175? **1**
How many tens are in the number 369? **6**

Page 146

Adding Three-Digit Numbers by Regrouping

Adding hundreds, tens, and ones sometimes involves regrouping. If the numbers in a column add up to more than 9, you need to regroup to the next higher place value.

Solve the problems by regrouping. Write the answers in the boxes below.

Hundreds	Tens	Ones
	1	
1	2	6
+ 1	4	7
2	7	3

Hundreds	Tens	Ones
		1
2	4	5
+ 5	3	7
7	8	2

Hundreds	Tens	Ones
		1
3	2	4
+ 4	3	7
7	6	1

Hundreds	Tens	Ones
	1	
4	6	5
+ 3	1	6
7	8	1

Hundreds	Tens	Ones
	1	
1	0	8
+ 8	1	3
9	2	1

Hundreds	Tens	Ones
	1	1
4	3	6
+ 3	6	5
8	0	1

Hundreds	Tens	Ones
	1	
5	3	6
+ 2	1	6
7	5	2

Hundreds	Tens	Ones
	1	1
2	7	9
+ 6	4	4
9	2	3

Hundreds	Tens	Ones
	1	1
2	5	6
+ 4	1	6
6	7	2

Solve the word problem and write the equation and the sum in the box.

Olivia is having a big party! She is buying party hats for everyone. She buys 178 silver party hats and 352 gold party hats. How many party hats did Olivia buy altogether?

Hundreds	Tens	Ones
1	1	
1	7	8
+ 3	5	2
5	3	0

Page 147

Adding Three-Digit Numbers with Regrouping Using Place Value

You can use place value to help you add multi-digit numbers when you need to regroup.

Example: 256 + 538 = 200 + 50 + 6
500 + 30 + 8
700 + 80 + 14 = 794

Solve the equations below by using the place-value strategy and write the answers on the lines.

126 + 147 =
100 + 20 + 6
100 + 40 + 7
200 + 60 + 13 = **273**

245 + 537 =
200 + 40 + 5
500 + 30 + 7
700 + 70 + 12 = **782**

708 + 213 =
700 + 0 + 8
200 + 10 + 3
900 + 10 + 11 = **921**

279 + 610 =
200 + 70 + 9
600 + 10 + 0
800 + 80 + 9 = **889**

324 + 437 =
300 + 20 + 4
400 + 30 + 7
700 + 50 + 11 = **761**

436 + 355 =
400 + 30 + 6
300 + 50 + 5
700 + 80 + 11 = **791**

Solve the word problem by using the place-value strategy and write the equation and the sum on the lines.

Alison is also having a big party! She has 178 red party hats and 312 blue party hats. How many hats does Alison have for her party?

100 + 70 + 8
300 + 10 + 2
400 + 80 + 10 = **490**

Page 148

Subtracting Three-Digit Numbers by Regrouping

Subtracting hundreds, tens, and ones sometimes involves regrouping. If the top number in a column is less than the bottom number, you need to regroup by borrowing from the next higher place value.

Solve the equations by regrouping. Write the differences in the boxes below.

Hundreds	Tens	Ones
	3	16
2	4̶	6̶
− 1	1	8
1	2	8

Hundreds	Tens	Ones
	1	12
4	2̶	2̶
− 3	1	4
1	0	8

Hundreds	Tens	Ones
4	0̶	13
8̶	1̶	3̶
− 4	3	5
0	7	8

Hundreds	Tens	Ones
6	0̶	14
7̶	1̶	4̶
− 5	3	7
1	7	7

Hundreds	Tens	Ones
	8	15
2	9̶	5̶
− 1	2	7
1	6	8

Hundreds	Tens	Ones
6	2̶	11
− 5	2	5
1	0	6

Hundreds	Tens	Ones
	0	13
8	1̶	3̶
− 3	0	5
8	0	8

Hundreds	Tens	Ones
	3	12
3	4̶	2̶
− 3	3	3
2	7	6

Hundreds	Tens	Ones
5	0̶	13
6̶	1̶	3̶
− 2	7	6
3	3	7

Solve the word problem and write the problem and the answer in the box.

Olivia needs to inflate 594 balloons for her party. She takes a break after inflating 276 balloons. How many balloons does she still need to inflate?

Hundreds	Tens	Ones
	8	14
5	9̶	4̶
− 2	7	6
3	1	8

Page 149

Adding to Check Subtraction

You can use related facts to help you check your answer to an addition or subtraction equation.

Think addition to check subtraction.

Example: If 435 − 123 = 312 then 312 + 123 = 435

Solve the subtraction equations and then check your answers using addition. Write the numbers on the lines below.

555 − 434 = **121**
121 + 434 = **555**

580 − 240 = **340**
340 + 240 = **580**

359 − 327 = **32**
32 + 327 = **359**

487 − 316 = **171**
171 + 316 = **487**

398 − 265 = **133**
133 + 265 = **398**

768 − 542 = **226**
226 + 542 = **768**

678 − 323 = **355**
355 + 323 = **678**

589 − 254 = **335**
335 + 254 = **589**

Solve the word problem and write the equation and the answer on the lines below.

Anthony and Rebecca collected 423 shells while walking on the beach. They gave Nicole 123 of them to start a collection of her own. How many seashells do Anthony and Rebecca still have in their collection?

423 − 123 = **300**
300 + 123 = **423**

Page 150

Addition and Subtraction Word Problems

Read each word problem carefully and look for clues to help you know if you should add or subtract. Numbers and words can be clues!

Circle the clues and use them to decide which operation and symbol you will use in your equation. Solve and write the answers on the lines below.

Will has 224 kayaks. He has rented 126 of them to a group of vacationers. How many kayaks have not been rented?

224 ⊖ 126 = **98**

Josh is picking apples from the orchard. He has picked 381 red ones and 160 green ones. How many apples does he have to make some apple pies?

381 ⊕ 160 = **541**

Jen and Rob took a lot of photos on vacation. Jen took 371 photos. Rob took 102 fewer photos than Jen. How many photos did Rob take?

371 ⊖ 102 = **269**

Alonzo sent postcards from Italy. He sent 216 postcards to friends and 116 to family members. How many postcards did he send while he was on vacation?

216 ⊕ 116 = **332**

Page 151

Multiplication Using a Model

Use the groups to help solve the multiplication equations. Write the products on the lines below.

How many flowers are there?
How many flowers are in each pot? How many pots are there?

2 flowers in each pot x **2** pots
2 x **2** = **4**

How much money is there?
How much is each coin worth? How many coins are there?

5 cents x **2** coins
5 x **2** = **10**

Circle the groups and multiply. Write the answers on the lines below.

4 groups of grasshoppers
x **3** in each group
4 x **3** = **12**

6 groups of inchworms
x **2** in each group
6 x **2** = **12**

2 groups of dragonflies
x **4** in each group
2 x **4** = **8**

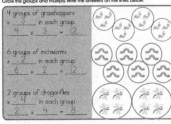

Page 152

Multiplication

Relate Addition to Multiplication Using Repeated Addition
You can use repeated addition to help you solve multiplication equations.

Example: There are 3 trees in the orchard.
Each tree has 4 apples.

4 + 4 + 4 = 12

3 × 4 = 12

Look at the groups in each of the illustrations below and use repeated addition to help you solve the multiplication equation.

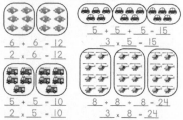

6 + 6 = 12
2 × 6 = 12

5 + 5 + 5 = 15
3 × 5 = 15

5 + 5 = 10
2 × 5 = 10

8 + 8 + 8 = 24
3 × 8 = 24

Page 153

Multiplication

Identity Property and Zero Property
The zero property of multiplication says that the product of 0 multiplied by any number is 0.

Example: 1 × 0 = 0 and 2 × 0 = 0
Solve the multiplication problems and write the answers in the boxes below.

3 × 0 = 0
10 × 0 = 0
4 × 0 = 0
7 × 0 = 0
6 × 0 = 0

5 × 0 = 0
8 × 0 = 0
1 × 0 = 0
6 × 0 = 0
9 × 0 = 0

The identity property of multiplication says that the product of 1 multiplied by any number is that number.

Example: 3 × 1 = 3 and 4 × 1 = 4
Solve the multiplication problems and write the answers in the boxes below.

3 × 1 = 3
9 × 1 = 9
6 × 1 = 6
8 × 1 = 8
2 × 1 = 2

5 × 1 = 5
7 × 1 = 7
1 × 1 = 1
4 × 1 = 4
10 × 1 = 10

Page 155

Multiplication

Find Unknowns
A letter can be used in place of an unknown factor. When a letter is used, it is known as a variable because its value varies when used in different equations. Use the multiplication table on page 154 to help you solve for the variable.

Example: n × 4 = 12

n = 3

s × 5 = 15   r × 2 = 12   8 × g = 56
3 × 5 = 15   6 × 2 = 12   8 × 7 = 56

7 × p = 70   9 × 9 = f   8 × 10 = h
7 × 10 = 70   9 × 9 = 81   8 × 10 = 80

5 × y = 45   r × 7 = 77   s × 9 = 36
5 × 9 = 45   11 × 7 = 77   4 × 9 = 36

8 × p = 72   6 × 4 = z   12 × w = 84
8 × 9 = 72   6 × 4 = 24   12 × 7 = 84

Page 156

Multiplication

Commutative Property
The commutative property of multiplication states that if you flip the order of the factors, the product will stay the same.

Example: 2 × 3 = 6 is the same as 3 × 2 = 6

Draw a small picture in the box to show the commutative property of multiplication. Then fill in the equation to solve.

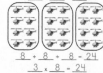

7 × 2 = 14   6 × 3 = 18   6 × 2 = 12   1 × 8 = 8
2 × 7 = 14   3 × 6 = 18   2 × 6 = 12   8 × 1 = 8

Associative Property
The associative property of multiplication states that when you have three or more factors, if the grouping of the factors changes, the product will stay the same. Use parentheses to group the factors.

Example: (2 × 3) × 5 = 2 × (3 × 5)
HINT: The factors didn't change. You still see 2, 3, and 5.

Use the associative property of multiplication to rewrite the equation another way. Then solve the multiplication equation.

3 × (2 × 2) =   4 × (1 × 3) =   (2 × 6) × 2 =
(3 × 2) × 2 =   (4 × 1) × 3 =   2 × (6 × 2) =
12   12   24

(1 × 7) × 5 =   5 × (3 × 1) =   (6 × 3) × 2 =
1 × (7 × 5) =   (5 × 3) × 1 =   6 × (3 × 2) =
35   15   36

Page 157

Multiplication

Arrays
You can create an array to help you solve multiplication equations. An array is a set that shows equal groups in rows and columns. By building an array, you can easily count the units to tell how many there are in all.

Example:

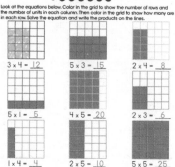

6 × 4
6 in each row
4 in each column

Look at the equations below. Color in the grid to show the number of rows and the number of units in each column. Then color in the grid to show how many are in each row. Solve the equation and write the products on the lines.

3 × 4 = 12   5 × 3 = 15   2 × 4 = 8

5 × 1 = 5   4 × 5 = 20   2 × 3 = 6

1 × 4 = 4   2 × 5 = 10   5 × 5 = 25

Page 158

Multiplication

Distributive Property Using Arrays
You can use the distributive property to break apart a multiplication equation with larger numbers into two smaller equations. By solving the two smaller equations and adding the products together, you will solve the larger equation.

Example:

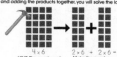

4 × 6   2 × 6 + 2 × 6 = 24

HINT: The number of rows stays the same.
Make the number in each row smaller.

Use orange to color in the square units to represent the multiplication equation. Use red to draw a line to break the array into two smaller pieces. Write the two multiplication equations you made based on your drawn red line in the parentheses below each grid. Solve by adding together the products and write your answer on the lines.

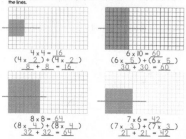

4 × 4 = 16   6 × 10 = 60
(4 × 2) + (4 × 2)   (6 × 5) + (6 × 5)
8 + 8 = 16   30 + 30 = 60

8 × 8 = 64   7 × 6 = 42
(8 × 4) + (8 × 4)   (7 × 3) + (7 × 3)
32 + 32 = 64   21 + 21 = 42

Page 159

Multiplication

Mixed Multiplication Practice
Practice multiplying by writing the products on the lines below.

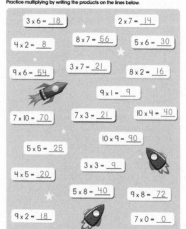

3 × 6 = 18   2 × 7 = 14
4 × 2 = 8   8 × 7 = 56   5 × 6 = 30
9 × 6 = 54   3 × 7 = 21   8 × 2 = 16
                  9 × 1 = 9
7 × 10 = 70   7 × 3 = 21   10 × 4 = 40
                  10 × 9 = 90
5 × 5 = 25   3 × 3 = 9
4 × 5 = 20   5 × 8 = 40   9 × 8 = 72
9 × 2 = 18   7 × 0 = 0

Page 160

Multiplication

Multiplying by Two and Three
Solve the multiplication equations and write the products in the boxes below. Use the multiplication table on page 154 if you need help.

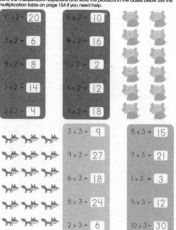

10 × 2 = 20   5 × 2 = 10
3 × 2 = 6   8 × 2 = 16
4 × 2 = 8   1 × 2 = 2
7 × 2 = 14   6 × 2 = 12
2 × 2 = 4   9 × 2 = 18

3 × 3 = 9   5 × 3 = 15
9 × 3 = 27   7 × 3 = 21
6 × 3 = 18   1 × 3 = 3
8 × 3 = 24   4 × 3 = 12
2 × 3 = 6   10 × 3 = 30

Page 161

Multiplication

Multiplying by Four and Five
Solve the multiplication equations and write the products in the boxes below. Use the multiplication table on page 154 if you need help.

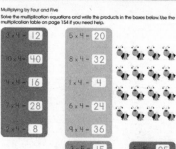

3 × 4 = 12   5 × 4 = 20
10 × 4 = 40   8 × 4 = 32
4 × 4 = 16   1 × 4 = 4
7 × 4 = 28   6 × 4 = 24
2 × 4 = 8   9 × 4 = 36

3 × 5 = 15   5 × 5 = 25
9 × 5 = 45   7 × 5 = 35
6 × 5 = 30   1 × 5 = 5
8 × 5 = 40   4 × 5 = 20
2 × 5 = 10   10 × 5 = 50

232

Page 162

Multiplication

Multiplying by Six and Seven

Solve the multiplication equations and write the products in the boxes below. Use the multiplication table on page 154 if you need help.

$3 \times 6 = 18$ $5 \times 6 = 30$

$10 \times 6 = 60$ $8 \times 6 = 48$

$4 \times 6 = 24$ $1 \times 6 = 6$

$7 \times 6 = 42$ $6 \times 6 = 36$

$2 \times 6 = 12$ $9 \times 6 = 54$

$3 \times 7 = 21$ $5 \times 7 = 35$

$9 \times 7 = 63$ $7 \times 7 = 49$

$6 \times 7 = 42$ $1 \times 7 = 7$

$8 \times 7 = 56$ $4 \times 7 = 28$

$2 \times 7 = 14$ $10 \times 7 = 70$

Page 163

Multiplication

Multiplying by Eight and Nine

Solve the multiplication equations and write the products in the boxes below. Use the multiplication table on page 154 if you need help.

$3 \times 8 = 24$ $5 \times 8 = 40$

$10 \times 8 = 80$ $8 \times 8 = 64$

$4 \times 8 = 32$ $7 \times 8 = 8$

$7 \times 8 = 56$ $6 \times 8 = 48$

$2 \times 8 = 16$ $9 \times 8 = 72$

$3 \times 9 = 27$ $5 \times 9 = 45$

$9 \times 9 = 81$ $7 \times 9 = 63$

$6 \times 9 = 54$ $1 \times 9 = 9$

$8 \times 9 = 72$ $4 \times 9 = 36$

$2 \times 9 = 18$ $10 \times 9 = 90$

Page 164

Multiplication

Multiplication Word Problems

When solving word problems, look for clues. Numbers and words are clues! Circle the numbers in the word problems and look for word clues. Hint: When a word problem has multiple groups to add, it means multiply.

Example: Rory walks ②miles to school every day. She goes to school ⑤times a week. How many miles does she walk in a school week?

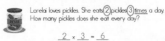
$2 \times 5 = 10$ miles

Circle the clues and solve the word problems. Write the products on the lines below.

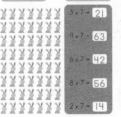 Lorelai loves pickles. She eats ②pickles ③times a day. How many pickles does she eat every day?

$2 \times 3 = 6$

 Kirk owns ⑤pairs of sunglasses. Patty owns ②times that amount. How many pairs of sunglasses does Patty own?

$5 \times 2 = 10$

 Richard bought ④boxes of cakes. Each box has ④cakes in it. How many total cakes does Richard have?

$4 \times 4 = 16$

Emily eats ③bunches of grapes. Each bunch has ⑩grapes. How many grapes did Emily eat?

$3 \times 10 = 30$

Page 165

Division

Exploring Division

Dividing means separating things into smaller groups.

Example: There are 8 hats altogether.
They are placed into 2 equal groups.
8 hats divided into 2 groups equals 4 hats in each group.
$8 \div 2 = 4$

Circle the objects and answer the questions to divide. Write the answers on the lines below.

How many shoes are there altogether? 10
Place the shoes into groups of 2 by circling equal sets.
How many groups are there? 5
$10 \div 2 = 5$

How many flowers are there altogether? 12
Place the flowers into groups of 3 by circling equal sets.
How many groups are there? 4
$12 \div 3 = 4$

How many gloves are there altogether? 20
Place the gloves into groups of 4 by circling equal sets.
How many groups are there? 5
$20 \div 4 = 5$

How many bows are there altogether? 15
Place the bows into groups of 5 by circling equal sets.
How many groups are there? 3
$15 \div 5 = 3$

Page 166

Division

Exploring Division

You can use an array to help you solve a division problem. In division you start with the whole set, known as the dividend. The divisor is one part of the dividend. The quotient is the answer (and the other part of the dividend). Use the arrays below to help you solve the problems. Write the quotients on the lines below.

How many apples are there altogether? 12
Place the apples into groups of 2 by circling equal sets.
How many groups are there? 6
$12 \div 2 = 6$

How many bananas are there altogether? 15
Place the bananas into groups of 3 by circling equal sets.
How many groups are there? 5
$15 \div 3 = 5$

How many pineapples are there altogether? 16
Place the pineapples into groups of 4 by circling equal sets.
How many groups are there? 4
$16 \div 4 = 4$

How many watermelons are there altogether? 10
Place the watermelons into groups of 5 by circling equal sets.
How many groups are there? 2
$10 \div 5 = 2$

Page 167

Division

Fact Families

Just like subtraction is related to addition, multiplication is related to division. You can use multiplication-related facts to help you solve division.

Example: If I know that $5 \times 6 = 30$, then $30 \div 5 = 6$

Use related facts and the properties of multiplication to help you fill in the multiplication and division fact families.

$4 \times 5 = 20$ $4 \times 6 = 24$
$5 \times 4 = 20$ $6 \times 4 = 24$
$20 \div 4 = 5$ $24 \div 6 = 4$
$20 \div 5 = 4$ $24 \div 4 = 6$

$9 \times 3 = 27$ $5 \times 2 = 10$
$3 \times 9 = 27$ $2 \times 5 = 10$
$27 \div 9 = 3$ $10 \div 5 = 2$
$27 \div 3 = 9$ $10 \div 2 = 5$

$2 \times 7 = 14$ $4 \times 7 = 28$
$2 \times 7 = 14$ $4 \times 7 = 28$
$14 \div 7 = 2$ $28 \div 7 = 4$
$14 \div 2 = 7$ $28 \div 4 = 7$

Page 168

Division

Division Word Problems

Circle the groups to help you divide. Then solve the division word problems and write the quotients on the lines below.

Annie has 8 flowerpots to give to her 4 friends. How many flowerpots will each friend get?
$8 \div 4 = 2$

Pat has 15 books to put into 3 boxes. How many books will go into each box?
$15 \div 3 = 5$

Katie has 12 cookies on a plate. She wants to share them equally with 4 friends. How many cookies will each friend get?
$12 \div 4 = 3$

Page 169

Fractions

Fractions

Fractions are parts of a whole number. Each piece represents a part of the whole.

Example: If a cookie is cut into two equal parts, each piece is $\frac{1}{2}$ of the whole cookie.

Fractions are expressed as a part over a whole. The part on top is known as the numerator. The numerator tells how many parts are shaded. The bottom number is known as the denominator. The denominator tells how many parts there are in the whole.

Example: $= \frac{1}{4}$ numerator / denominator

The 1 represents how many parts are shaded.
The 4 represents how many parts there are in the whole shape.

Write the missing numerators or denominators for the fractions shown below.

$\frac{4}{8}$ $\frac{1}{2}$

$\frac{3}{4}$ $\frac{1}{3}$

$\frac{5}{8}$ $\frac{1}{5}$

Page 170

Fractions

Fractions

Color the parts of the shapes to match the fractions.

$\frac{1}{2}$ $\frac{5}{8}$

$\frac{2}{4}$ $\frac{1}{3}$

$\frac{3}{4}$ $\frac{2}{6}$

$\frac{2}{6}$ $\frac{6}{10}$

Page 171

Fractions

Fractions on a Number Line

You can use a number line to show fractions. The length or distance from one whole number to the next whole number represents one whole. The number line can be broken into any number of equal parts.

Example: Drew's family is traveling from his house to his aunt May's farm. They stop at a gas station when they are $\frac{3}{4}$ of the way there.

Drew's House   Aunt May's Farm

$\frac{3}{4}$ is 3 out of 4 equal parts. By counting forward 3 parts starting with 0, you can mark the fraction on the number line.

Break each number line below into equal parts based on each fraction's denominator. Write each fraction on the number line and then place a dot on the correct fraction. HINT: The denominator, or bottom number, tells you how many equal parts there will be in all.

If a number line is partitioned into eighths, how many equal parts are there? 8

If a number line is partitioned into fourths, how many equal parts are there? 4

Page 172

Fractions

Fractions on a Number Line
Look at the number lines below to answer the questions.

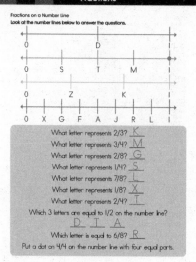

What letter represents 2/3? K
What letter represents 3/4? M
What letter represents 2/8? G
What letter represents 1/4? S
What letter represents 7/8? L
What letter represents 1/8? X
What letter represents 2/4? T
Which 3 letters are equal to 1/2 on the number line?
D T A
Which letter is equal to 6/8? R
Put a dot on 4/4 on the number line with four equal parts.

Page 173

Fractions

Compare Fractions
Just like you can compare whole numbers, you can also compare fractions.

Example: Sue ate 3/6 of her cookie, and Bob ate 5/6 of his cookie.
Who ate more of their cookie?

Sue's Cookie   Bob ate more of his cookie than Sue.   Bob's Cookie
3/6 < 5/6

Color in the shapes to match the fractions. Then look at the fractions and use <, >, or = to compare the two "parts to whole" amounts.

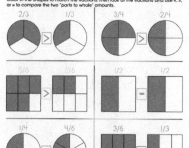

2/3 > 1/3   3/4 > 2/4
5/6 > 2/6   1/2 = 1/2
1/4 < 4/6   3/6 > 1/3

Page 174

Measurement

Measuring Length
An inch can be written like this: in. It is used to measure short lengths.

A foot can be written like this: ft. It is used to measure longer lengths.

A mile can be written like this: mi. It is used to measure very long lengths.

An estimate is a thoughtful guess. Sometimes we need to make a thoughtful guess about how long something is.

Look at the pictures below and circle the unit of measurement that would be best for measuring each REAL object.

(in.) ft.   ft. (mi.)   (ft.) mi.
(in.) ft.   (in.) mi.   in. (ft.)
ft. (in.)   mi. (ft.)   in. (mi.)

Page 175

Measurement

Measuring Length
Measure the objects using the ruler. Write the measured lengths on the lines below.

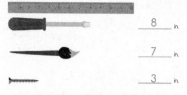

8 in.
7 in.
3 in.

Read the word problems and circle or write the answers below.

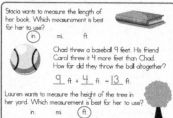

Stacia wants to measure the length of her book. Which measurement is best for her to use?
(in.)   mi.   ft.

Chad threw a baseball 9 feet. His friend Carol threw it 4 more feet than Chad. How far did they throw the ball altogether?
9 ft + 4 ft = 13 ft.

Lauren wants to measure the height of the tree in her yard. Which measurement is best for her to use?
in.   mi.   (ft.)

Page 176

Measurement

Capacity
If you want to know how much a container holds (for example, how much water a swimming pool can hold), you want to know its capacity.

A liter can be written like this: L.
It is used to measure large containers, such as a pool or a bathtub.
A milliliter can be written like this: mL.
It is used to measure small containers, such as a spoon or measuring cup.

1 liter = 1000 milliliters   and $\frac{1}{2}$ liter = 500 milliliters

Color each container to the correct measurement in milliliters.

100 ml   300 ml   700 ml   1 L   400 ml

Do these containers hold more or less than a liter? Check the box with the correct answer for each container.

cup	☐ more than / ☑ less than	truck (oil)	☑ more than / ☐ less than
paper	☑ more than / ☐ less than	MILK	☑ more than / ☐ less than

---

Page 177

Measurement

Capacity
You can use what you know about fractions to measure capacities.

Example:

$\frac{1}{4}$ (1 quarter) $\frac{1}{2}$ (1 half) $\frac{3}{4}$ (3 quarters)   full

Color each of the glasses with a yellow colored pencil to give each person the amount of lemonade he or she wants.

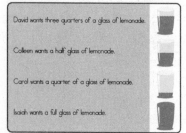

David wants three quarters of a glass of lemonade.

Colleen wants a half glass of lemonade.

Carol wants a quarter of a glass of lemonade.

Isaiah wants a full glass of lemonade.

Word Problem
If a plastic pool holds 20 liters of water, how many 5 liter buckets of water will you need to use to fill it up?
20 ÷ 5 = 4

20 liters   5 liters

Page 178

Measurement

Mass
Mass is a measurement of how much matter is in an object. Mass is measured in kilograms (kg) or grams (g). Kilograms measure objects with larger masses. Grams measure objects with smaller masses.

Example: The mass of a kitten is about 2 kg.
The mass of a diamond ring is about 1.5 g.
The mass of an apple is about 100 g.

If both things on either end of a scale have the same mass, the scale will balance. Write the mass of the food items in the boxes below.

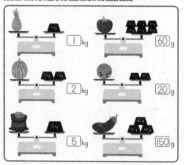

1 kg   60 g
2 kg   20 g
5 kg   150 g

Page 179

Time

Time to the Minute
The minute hand tells how many minutes have passed in an hour. In 1 minute, the minute hand moves from one hash mark to the next. Every time the minute hand moves from one whole number to the next, it has been 5 minutes. Skip count by fives and then count forward one for each hash mark to tell how many minutes after the hour have passed.

Example: The hour hand is past 3 but not yet near 4.
The minute hand is 2 marks past 15, so it is 3:17.

What time is it? Write the time under each clock.

2:23   10:12   4:36
3:44   11:51   6:05

What time is it? Draw the hands on the clocks to match the digital times.

5:07   3:59   6:16

Page 180

Time

A.M. and P.M.

Writing a.m. or p.m. after a time lets you know if it is daytime or nighttime. You use a.m. for anytime from midnight to midday, or noon. You use p.m. for anytime from midday, or noon, until midnight. You can use a number line to think about time as distance. It can also help you think about the number of hours in a day. There are twelve hours in the a.m. and twelve hours in the p.m. A day is twenty-four hours.

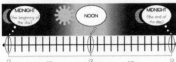

Think about the activities and the time on the clock. Then write the time for the activity on the lines below using a.m. or p.m.

Ride a bicycle **p.m.**   Eat dinner **p.m.**   Make eggs **a.m.**

Go to bed **p.m.**   Go to school **a.m.**   Play baseball **p.m.**

Quarter after 8 in the morning **8:15 a.m.**
8 minutes after 7 in the evening **7:08 p.m.**
AJ has practice 22 minutes after 4 in the afternoon. **4:22 p.m.**
Luca eats breakfast at half past 7 in the morning. **7:30 a.m.**
Nolen leaves for school 25 minutes before 8 in the morning. **7:35 a.m.**
Huxley feeds Pepper at quarter after 5 in the evening. **5:15 p.m.**

Page 181

Time

Elapsed Time

Elapsed time means how much time has passed. You can use a number line to help you figure out elapsed time.

Example: Ashton started baseball practice at 4:30 p.m. His practice ended at 6:15 p.m. How long was Ashton's practice? HINT: There are 60 minutes in an hour.

+60   +30   +15   = 105 min. or 1 hour and 45 min.
or 1 HOUR

Read each word problem carefully. Use the number line to help you figure out the elapsed time. Start by creating the hash marks you need to represent the span of time. Then draw your arrows and write the amount of elapsed time on the lines below.

Sarah started her homework at 3:15 p.m. She finished all of her homework at 4:30 p.m. How long did it take Sarah to finish her homework? **1 hour 15 minutes**

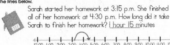

Kelly went to the mall at 10:30 a.m. She got home at 12:15 p.m. How long did Kelly shop at the mall? **1 hour 45 minutes**

Morgan went for a run. He left the house at 5:25 a.m. Morgan finished his run at 7:20 a.m. How long did he run this morning? **1 hour 55 minutes**

Page 182

Data Management

Reading a Scaled Bar Graph

Reading a scaled bar graph means counting the numbers each bar represents and analyzing the data. Scaled bar graphs mean that the number of each unit of measure will represent more than one. In the graph below, the scale increment is by fives.

Look at the scaled bar graph and answer the questions. Write the answers on the lines below.

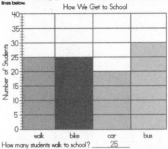
How We Get to School

How many students walk to school? **25**
How many students ride their bikes to school? **25**
Do more students take the bus or ride in a car? **bus**
How many students altogether walk or ride their bikes? **50**
What is the most popular way to get to school? **bus**
What is the least popular way to get to school? **car**

Page 183

Data Management

Making a Scaled Bar Graph

Use the tally graph data to make a scaled bar graph. Then answer the questions. Write the answers on the lines below.

jumping rope	𝍷𝍷 𝍷𝍷 𝍷𝍷
playing sports	𝍷𝍷 𝍷𝍷 𝍷𝍷 𝍷𝍷
reading a book	𝍷𝍷 𝍷𝍷 𝍷𝍷𝍷𝍷
talking with friends	𝍷𝍷 𝍷𝍷𝍷
swinging	𝍷𝍷

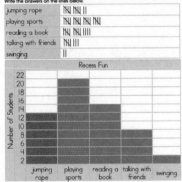
Recess Fun

How many kids like jumping rope at recess? **12**
How many kids like reading a book? **14**
What is the most popular recess activity? **playing sports**
What is the least popular recess activity? **swinging**
How many kids voted altogether? **56**

Page 184

Geometry

Congruent Shapes

Congruent shapes are figures that are the same size and same shape.

Are the shapes below congruent? Circle yes or no.

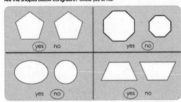

yes (no)   yes (no)

yes (no)   (yes) no

Color the congruent figures orange.

Draw two figures that are congruent in the box below.

Page 185

Geometry

Plane Figures

A plane figure is a figure that is formed on a flat surface. It is formed by points that make line segments, curved paths, or both.

Example: A point marks an exact location.

Endpoints are used to show segments of a line.

A line segment is straight, a part of a line and has two endpoints.

A line is a straight path that continues in both directions and does not end.

A ray is straight, part of a line, has one end point, and continues on in one direction.

A curved path will have a bend in its line.

A closed shape starts and ends at the same point.

An open shape does not start and end at the same point.

Write how many line segments each figure has on the lines below.

6   **6**   **4**   **4**   **8**

Look at the figures below and write whether the figures are open or closed.

open   **closed**   **closed**   **open**   **closed**

Page 186

Geometry

Angles

An angle is formed when two line segments share the same endpoint. A right angle is an angle that forms a square corner. Some angles can be less than a right angle, and some angles can be greater than a right angle.

right angle

Use the corner of a piece of paper to help you determine whether the angles on the figures below are right angles, less than right angles, or greater than right angles. Write your answer on the lines.

right   **greater than right**   **right**

less than right   **right**   **less than right**

Look at the shapes below. Write how many right angles each shape has on the lines below.

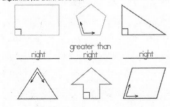

5   **8**

Page 187

Geometry

Identifying Polygons

A polygon is any two-dimensional figure with three or more sides. That means there are a lot of different kinds of polygons!

Oftentimes, a figure is named for the number of sides and number of angles it has in total.

Example: A triangle has **3** sides and angles.   "Tri" means three.

A quadrilateral has **4** sides and angles.   "Quad" means four.

A pentagon has **5** sides and angles.   "Penta" means five.

A hexagon has **6** sides and angles.   "Hexa" means six.

A heptagon has **7** sides and angles.   "Hepta" means seven.

An octagon has **8** sides and angles.   "Octa" means eight.

Write how many sides and angles each polygon has on the lines below.

6 sides   **7** sides   **3** sides
5 angles   **6** angles   **3** angles

Page 188

Perimeter

Perimeter

Perimeter is the distance around a figure. If you walked along an entire fence surrounding a horse in a field, you could say, "I walked the perimeter, and now I am tired!"

Example: What is the fence perimeter around the horse in this field? You can find the perimeter by adding together the length of each side. The rectangular fence has four sides.
A rectangle has two sides that are parallel and the same length. In order to find the perimeter, you need to add the two missing side lengths.
Add 4 ft. + 7 ft. + 4 ft. + 7 ft. = 22 ft.
11 ft. + 11 ft. = 22 ft.
The fence perimeter is 22 feet long.

Fill in the missing lengths and then find the perimeter of each figure. Be sure to include the units in your answer.

Perimeter: **16 yd**   Perimeter: **22 in.**   Perimeter: **16 ft.**

HINT: A square has four sides that are all the same length.

Perimeter: **16 in.**   Perimeter: **32 ft.**   Perimeter: **8 in.**

Solve the perimeter word problems below. Write your answers on the lines.

A rectangle has a side that is 5 inches long and a side that is 7 inches long. What is the perimeter of the rectangle? **24 in.**

A square has a side that is 8 feet long. What is the perimeter of the square? **32 ft.**

Perimeter

Polygon Perimeters
Find the perimeter of the polygons below. Remember that to find the perimeter, you need to add each side of the polygon together.
Find the perimeter of the figures below. Be sure to include the units in your answer.

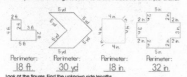
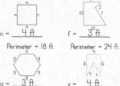

Perimeter: Perimeter: Perimeter: Perimeter:
__18 ft.__   __30 yd__   __18 in.__   __32 in__

Look at the figures. Find the unknown side lengths.

Perimeter = 16 ft.   Perimeter = 32 ft.

n = __4 ft.__   f = __3 ft.__

Perimeter = 18 ft.   Perimeter = 24 ft.

g = __3 ft.__   x = __4 ft.__

Solve the perimeter word problems below. Write your answers on the lines.

A pencil case has a height of 7 inches and a width of 4 inches. What is the perimeter of the pencil case? __22 in.__

Ellie got an envelope in the mail. It had a height of 8 inches and a width of 5 inches. What is the perimeter of the envelope? __26 in.__

Area

Area
You have learned that perimeter is the distance around a figure. Area is the measurement of the number of square units used to cover a surface. For example, builders need to know how many square units there are in a kitchen floor to make sure they have enough wood to cover the entire floor area.

Unit Square

Example: You can find area by counting the number of square units. This figure has an area of 3 sq. units.

Draw lines to make square units inside each figure. Then count the square units to find the area of the figures below. Write the answer on the lines.

Area = __18__ square units   Area = __7__ square units   Area = __9__ square units

Area = __12__ square units   Area = __16__ square units

Area = __18__ square units

Write area or perimeter for each situation.

Carpeting a floor: __area__   Putting tile on a bathroom wall __area__

Fencing a garden __perimeter__   Enclosing a playground in a backyard __perimeter__

Area

Relate Multiplication to Area
A more efficient way to find the area of a figure is by using multiplication. You can use what you know about arrays in multiplication to help you figure out the area.

Example: This rectangle is like an array. ← row

1. Count the number of rows. 3
2. Count how many units are in each row. 4

You can now multiply how many square units are in each row by the number of rows.

3 × 4 = 12, so the area of this rectangle is 12 square units.

Find the area of the figures below. Write the multiplication equation and the area on the lines.

__3__ × __8__ = __24__   __4__ × __4__ = __16__   __4__ × __6__ = __24__
Area = __24__ sq. units   Area = __16__ sq. units   Area = __24__ sq. units

The city is planning a new park. The area for the playground is 8 units wide by 4 units long. How many square units is the area for the playground?

__32__ square units

Greg helps his dad build a chicken coop that is 6 yards long by 2 yards wide. How many square yards long will the chicken coop be?

__12__ square yards

Word Problems

Two-Step Word Problems
Sometimes word problems have more than one step to solve before answering the question. When reading a word problem, try to picture what is happening in your mind to help you know what different steps you need to take.

Example: Kelly went to the department store. She bought 2 shirts that cost $12 each. When Kelly started shopping, she had $42. How much money did she have left after she bought the shirts?

STEP 1: How much money did she spend on the shirts? She bought 2 shirts, and each shirt cost $12. To solve the first step, you need to add 12 + 12 or multiply 12 × 2. Kelly spent $24.

STEP 2: Kelly started with $42. If she spent money, that means you need to subtract to take that money away from her original amount of money. $42 − $24 = $18

The final answer is Kelly has $18 left after buying two shirts.

Read each word problem carefully. Complete each step that is needed and show your work. Write your answers below.

Derek had 3 packs of baseball cards. Each pack had 10 cards. He gave 8 cards to his friends. How many cards does Derek still have?
3 × 10 = 30   30 − 8 = 22   22

Joey baked 36 cookies. His dad ate 12 of his cookies. Joey then gave his friend some cookies. He now has 10 cookies left. How many cookies did he give his friend?
36 − 12 = 24   24 − 10 = 14   14

Avery has 42 markers in her box. She gave 3 friends 3 markers each. How many markers does Avery have left?
3 × 3 = 9   42 − 9 = 33   33

Word Problems

Two-Step Word Problems
Read each word problem carefully. Complete each step that is needed and show your work. Write your answers below.

Scott bought 4 books from the bookstore. Each book cost $5. He also bought a backpack for $8. How much money did Scott spend?
4 × $5 = $20
$20 + $8 = $28 $28

Troy made 15 bracelets. He gave 2 bracelets each to 2 friends. How many bracelets does Troy have left?
2 × 2 = 4
15 − 4 = 11   11

Grady has 20 toy cars. He buys 15 more cars from the store. Grady gave 6 cars to his brother. How many toy cars does Grady have now?
20 + 15 = 35
35 − 6 = 29   29

Ed planted a garden. He planted 3 rows of corn with 6 seeds in each row. He then planted 12 bean seeds. How many seeds did Ed plant?
3 × 6 = 18
18 + 12 = 30   30

Brady has 4 packs of candy. Each pack has 11 candies in it. Brady gives 10 candies to his friend. How many candies does Brady have left?
4 × 11 = 44
44 − 10 = 34   34

Laura has 42 beads. She makes 4 bracelets. Each bracelet has 6 beads on it. How many beads does Laura still have to make more bracelets?
4 × 6 = 24
42 − 24 = 18   18

Vocabulary

Syllables
Read the words below out loud as you clap each syllable. How many syllables do you hear? Sort the words into the correct categories based on the number of claps you hear. Write them on the lines below.

tangerine   peach   banana   papaya   orange   lime
apple   pear   mango   cherry   lemon   strawberry

1 SYLLABLE	2 SYLLABLES	3 SYLLABLES
peach	apple	tangerine
orange	mango	banana
lime	cherry	papaya
pear	lemon	strawberry

Vocabulary

Look up the words below in a dictionary. Write the definition on the lines below.

assist
to help someone

fossil
the remains of a prehistoric organism preserved in rock

absorb
take in or soak up

imaginary
existing in one's imagination

climate
the weather conditions in an area

project
an activity that is planned to achieve a certain goal

routine
a sequence of actions followed regularly

essential
something that is necessary or important

Reading Comprehension

Facts and Opinions
Read each sentence below and determine if it is a fact or an opinion. Circle the correct answer.

Orange juice tastes better than apple juice.	fact	(opinion)
Multiplication is easier than addition.	fact	(opinion)
Watermelon is a type of fruit.	(fact)	opinion
Snow only falls when the temperature is cold enough.	(fact)	opinion
Plants need sunlight to grow.	(fact)	opinion
Reading is more fun than playing basketball.	fact	(opinion)
The sun is out during the day.	(fact)	opinion
Everybody likes broccoli.	fact	(opinion)
Being a chef is harder than being a doctor.	fact	(opinion)
Penguins can't fly.	(fact)	opinion
August has thirty-one days.	(fact)	opinion
Summer should be longer.	fact	(opinion)

Write one sentence that is a fact.

_____

Write one sentence that is your opinion.

_____

Reading Comprehension

Making Predictions
Read the sentences below and circle what you predict will come next.   100

I forgot to do my homework, and I...
a. received a bad grade.   b. went to lunch.   c. got a new toy.

My dad packed me two pudding cups, so I...
a. missed lunch.   b. got sent home early.   c. gave one to my friend.

There is a lot of snow outside, so...
a. it must be Tuesday.   b. school might be canceled.   c. my mom will mow the lawn.

After I got a 100 on my spelling test, I felt...
a. tired.   b. hungry.   c. happy.

If I don't take out the trash...
a. I will see my cousins.   b. our house will start to smell bad.   c. my dog will eat her food.

Because we're going to the pool...
a. I put on sunscreen.   b. I put on my winter coat.   c. I did laundry.

Page 202

Grammar

better	more expensive	taller	as often as
more	more carefully	shorter	as perfectly as

Read each sentence below. Use the comparative adverbs in the table above to complete the sentences.

1. A gorilla eats ___more___ food than a cat.

2. My dad is ___taller___ than me.

3. The cake isn't decorated ___as perfectly as___ this one.

4. My sister is ___better___ at video games than I am.

5. This sweater is ___more expensive___ than this coat.

6. I cut the paper ___more carefully___ than last time.

7. My friend doesn't bring sandwiches for lunch ___as often as___ I do.

8. An inch is ___shorter___ than a foot.

Page 203

Grammar

smartest	most important	least favorite	last
funniest	most popular	least spicy	first

Read each sentence below. Use the superlative adverbs in the table above to complete the sentences.

1. The cartoon with the talking pineapple is the ___funniest___ show on TV.

2. A hamster is the ___most popular___ class pet.

3. Bell pepper is the ___least spicy___ type of pepper.

4. Breakfast is the ___most important___ meal of the day.

5. My teacher is the ___smartest___ person I know.

6. The ___last___ thing I do before bed is brush my teeth.

7. Oranges are my ___least favorite___ fruit.

8. Our project came ___first___ in the science fair.

Page 204

Writing Sentences

Writing Complex Sentences

For each sentence below:
- circle the independent clause in red
- circle the dependent clause in blue
- put a box around the subordinating conjunction in purple

My mom gave me an ice-cream cone [because] I got a 100 on my multiplication test.

[If you come to my birthday party,] we can play hide-and-seek.

[Even though] I'm younger than him I'm better at board games than my brother.

I can't go to the movies [unless] I do my homework.

My sister packed my lunch [while] I tied my shoes.

Page 205

Writing Sentences

Read the sentences in the blue box below. Rewrite the sentences using the dialogue rules. Hint: There will be four paragraphs. Look at page 97 if you need help remembering the dialogue rules.

Maria gave me half of her sandwich, and she said, Can I have half of yours? Okay, I said, but then I get half of your cookie! Deal, she said. She gave me half of her cookie. I can't wait to eat this, I said, I'm starving!

Maria gave me half of her sandwich, and she said, "Can I have half of yours?"

"Okay," I said, "but then I get half of your cookie!"

"Deal," she said. She gave me half of her cookie.

"I can't wait to eat this," I said. "I'm starving!"

Page 206

The Writing Process

Revising and Editing Writing

Read the passage. Use the checklist and proofreading marks from page 101 to help revise and edit this draft. Then draw a picture to match the passage below.

We Deserve More Recess

I think weas students deserve to have recess for an extra our on fridays. children need too be active to help exercise there growing muscles. My teacher, mr. Gary agrees. He told me if students don't exercise enough, they will get distracted during class. In conclusion, I think recess needs to be longer on Fridays.

Page 211

Number Sense

Least to Greatest

Put the numbers in order from least to greatest. Write the numbers on the lines below.

1,126 4,019 3,343 6,202	1,126 3,343 4,019 6,202
2,004 7,207 1,080 5,413	1,080 2,004 5,413 7,207
8,320 3,111 6,020 1,337	1,337 3,111 6,020 8,320
4,612 2,104 2,982 5,508	2,104 2,982 4,612 5,508
1,357 9,400 8,642 9,450	1,357 8,642 9,400 9,450

Use the models below to count and write how many thousands, hundreds, tens, and ones there are on the lines below.

__1__ thousand + __5__ hundreds + __5__ tens + __8__ ones = __1,558__

__2__ thousands + __1__ hundred + __4__ tens + __7__ ones = __2,147__

__3__ thousands + __2__ hundreds + __2__ tens + __1__ one = __3,221__

Page 212

Number Sense

Use the number line to help you round. Read the numbers and mark them on the number lines with a dot. Then round to the nearest ten and write your answers on the lines below.

__10__   __40__

__90__   __70__

Round to the nearest ten. Write the answers on the lines.

92 __90__   42 __40__   35 __40__   65 __70__

Use the number line to help you round. Read the numbers and mark them on the number lines with a dot. Then round to the nearest hundred and write your answer on the lines below.

__200__   __300__

__400__   __800__

Round to the nearest hundred. Write the answers on the lines below.

874 __900__   563 __600__   218 __200__   604 __600__

The lion weighs 287 pounds. What is its weight rounded to the nearest hundred pounds? __300__ pounds

Page 213

Addition and Subtraction

Adding Three-Digit Numbers by Regrouping

Adding hundreds, tens, and ones sometimes involves regrouping. If the numbers in a column add up to more than 9, you need to regroup to the next higher place value.

Solve the problems by regrouping. Write the answers in the boxes below.

Hundreds	Tens	Ones
		1
2	4	8
+ 1	3	5
3	8	3

Hundreds	Tens	Ones
		1
3	8	2
+ 4	5	9
8	4	1

Hundreds	Tens	Ones
4	0	4
+ 3	9	8
8	0	2

Hundreds	Tens	Ones
	1	
7	1	9
+ 1	4	3
8	6	2

Hundreds	Tens	Ones
	1	
5	5	6
+ 1	5	3
7	0	9

Hundreds	Tens	Ones
	1	
8	2	7
+ 1	4	4
9	7	1

Hundreds	Tens	Ones
1		
6	3	4
+ 1	6	6
8	0	0

Hundreds	Tens	Ones
1		
7	1	1
+ 2	1	9
9	3	0

Hundreds	Tens	Ones
1	1	
3	8	9
+ 4	9	8
8	8	7

Solve the word problem and write the equation and the sum in the box.

Ari is practicing for a baking competition. She has baked 237 cookies and 486 cupcakes so far. How much food has she baked in all?

Hundreds	Tens	Ones
1	1	
2	3	7
+ 4	8	6
7	2	3

Page 214

Addition and Subtraction

Adding Three-Digit Numbers with Regrouping Using Place Value

You can use place value to help you add multi-digit numbers when you need to regroup.

Solve the equations below by using the place-value strategy and write the answers on the lines.

804 + 128 =
800 + 0 + 4
100 + 20 + 8
900 + 20 + 12 = 932

705 + 219 =
700 + 0 + 5
200 + 10 + 9
900 + 10 + 14 = 924

416 + 338 =
400 + 10 + 6
300 + 30 + 8
700 + 40 + 14 = 754

227 + 167 =
200 + 20 + 7
100 + 60 + 7
300 + 80 + 14 = 394

514 + 379 =
500 + 10 + 4
300 + 70 + 9
800 + 80 + 13 = 893

621 + 149 =
600 + 20 + 1
100 + 40 + 9
700 + 60 + 10 = 770

Solve the word problem by using the place-value strategy and write the equation and the sum on the lines.

Clarissa is also practicing for the baking competition. She has baked 207 pies and 486 muffins. How much food has she baked in all?

200 + 0 + 7
400 + 80 + 6
600 + 80 + 13 = 693

Page 215

Addition and Subtraction

Subtracting Three-Digit Numbers by Regrouping
Subtracting hundreds, tens, and ones sometimes involves regrouping. If the top number in a column is less than the bottom number, you need to regroup by borrowing from the next highest place value.
Solve the equations by regrouping. Write the differences in the boxes below.

Hundreds	Tens	Ones
6	2̶ 12	11
7̶	3̶	1̶
- 2	3	7
4	9	4

Hundreds	Tens	Ones
	1	15
6	2̶	5̶
- 3	1	7
3	0	8

Hundreds	Tens	Ones
8	2̶ 12	10
9̶	3̶	0̶
- 3	7	2
5	5	8

Hundreds	Tens	Ones
3	10̶	13
4̶	1̶	3̶
- 1	3	6
2	7	7

Hundreds	Tens	Ones
4	14̶	15
5̶	5̶	5̶
- 2	8	7
2	6	8

Hundreds	Tens	Ones
5	2̶	11
8̶	3̶	1̶
- 4	4	4
1	7	7

Hundreds	Tens	Ones
	2	10
9̶	3̶	0̶
- 3	0	2
6	2	8

Hundreds	Tens	Ones
1	0̶	10
2̶	1̶	0̶
- 1	3	6
0	7	4

Hundreds	Tens	Ones
	6	14
7̶	4̶	4̶
- 2	0	9
1	6	5

Solve the word problem and write the problem and the answer in the box.

Eliza is writing a 550-word essay for school. She has already written 317 words. How many words does she have left to write?

Hundreds	Tens	Ones
	4	10
5	5̶	0̶
- 3	1	7
2	3	3

Page 216

Addition and Subtraction

Addition and Subtraction Word Problems
Read each word problem carefully and look for clues to help you decide if you should add or subtract. Numbers and words can be clues!
Circle the clues and use them to decide which operation and symbol you will use in your equation. Solve and write the answers on the lines below.

Lottie and Javier had to draw circles for an art project. Javier drew 138 circles. Lottie drew 214 (more) circles than Javier. How many circles did Lottie draw?

138 ⊕ 214 = 352

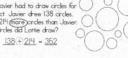

Clare had 763 marbles. She gave 414 marbles to Eli. How many marbles does Clare (have left)?

763 ⊖ 414 = 349

Eduardo and Mac both collect trading cards. Eduardo has 525 cards. Mac has 138 (fewer) cards than Eduardo. How many cards does Mac have?

525 ⊖ 138 = 387

Meredith collects flowers. She has 320 roses and 605 daisies. How many flowers does she have (altogether)?

320 ⊕ 605 = 925

Page 217

Multiplication

Look at the groups in each of the illustrations below and use repeated addition to help you solve the multiplication equation.

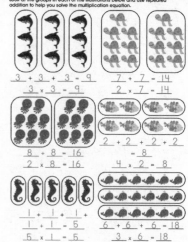

3 + 3 + 3 = 9
3 × 3 = 9

7 + 7 = 14
2 × 7 = 14

8 + 8 = 16
2 × 8 = 16

2 + 2 + 2 + 2 = 8
4 × 2 = 8

1 + 1 + 1 + 1 + 1 = 5
5 × 1 = 5

6 + 6 + 6 = 18
3 × 6 = 18

Page 218

Multiplication

Find Unknowns
A letter can be used in place of an unknown factor. When a letter is used, it is known as a variable because its value varies when used in different equations.
Use the multiplication table on page 154 if you need help solving for the variable.

Example:

$n \times 4 = 12$

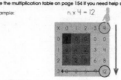

$n = 3$

$6 \times v = 36$
$6 \times 6 = 36$

$10 \times 4 = k$
$10 \times 4 = 40$

$a \times 7 = 35$
$5 \times 7 = 35$

$3 \times 9 = d$
$3 \times 9 = 27$

$4 \times t = 20$
$4 \times 5 = 20$

$8 \times 0 = m$
$8 \times 0 = 0$

$i \times 8 = 64$
$8 \times 8 = 64$

$q \times 7 = 63$
$9 \times 7 = 63$

$6 \times u = 66$
$6 \times 11 = 66$

$6 \times 12 = c$
$6 \times 12 = 72$

$n \times 2 = 18$
$9 \times 2 = 18$

$7 \times e = 49$
$7 \times 7 = 49$

Page 219

Division

Exploring Division
You can use an array to help you solve a division problem. In division, start with the whole set, known as the dividend. The divisor is one part of the dividend. The quotient is the answer (and the other part of the dividend). Use the arrays below to help solve the problems. Write the quotients on the lines below.

How many juice boxes are there altogether? 25
Place the juice boxes into groups of 5 by circling equal sets.
How many groups are there? 5
25 ÷ 5 = 5

How many cupcakes are there altogether? 24
Place the cupcakes into groups of 4 by circling equal sets.
How many groups are there? 6
24 ÷ 4 = 6

How many cookies are there altogether? 30
Place the cookies into groups of 10 by circling equal sets.
How many groups are there? 3
30 ÷ 10 = 3

How many ice-cream cones are there altogether? 24
Place the ice-cream cones into groups of 8 by circling equal sets.
How many groups are there? 3
24 ÷ 8 = 3

Page 220

Fractions

Fractions
Color the parts of the shapes to match the fractions.

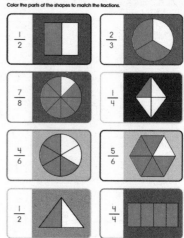

$\frac{1}{2}$

$\frac{2}{3}$

$\frac{7}{8}$

$\frac{1}{4}$

$\frac{4}{6}$

$\frac{5}{6}$

$\frac{1}{2}$

$\frac{4}{4}$

Page 221

Fractions

Break each number line into equal parts based on each fraction's denominator. Write each fraction on the number line and then place a dot on the correct fraction. HINT: The denominator, or bottom number, tells you how many equal parts there will be in all.

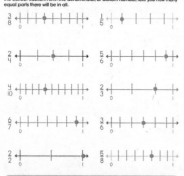

$\frac{3}{8}$

$\frac{1}{5}$

$\frac{2}{4}$

$\frac{5}{6}$

$\frac{4}{10}$

$\frac{2}{3}$

$\frac{6}{7}$

$\frac{3}{6}$

$\frac{2}{2}$

$\frac{5}{8}$

If a number line is partitioned into fifths, how many equal parts are there? 5

If a number line is partitioned into thirds, how many equal parts are there? 3

Page 222

Time

What time is it? Write the time under each clock.

8:16   5:27   7:47

1:54   9:33   12:03

What time is it? Draw the hands on the clocks to match the digital times.

1:37   11:02   7:56

4:44   10:20   2:18

Page 223

Data Management

Making a Scaled Bar Graph
Use the tally graph data to make a scaled bar graph. Then answer the questions.
Write the answers on the lines below.

mystery	||||| ||||| ||||
adventure	||||| ||||| ||||| |||||
fantasy	||||| ||||| ||||
biographies	||||
picture books	||||| ||||| ||

Types of Books

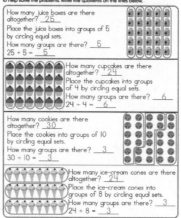

(bar graph; y-axis: Number of Students, values 2 to 22; x-axis: mystery, adventure, fantasy, biographies, picture books)

How many kids like fantasy books? 14
How many kids like picture books? 12
What kind of book is the most popular? adventure
What kind of book is the least popular? biographies
How many kids voted altogether? 64

Geometry

Write how many line segments each figure has on the lines below.

5   6   10   3   12

Look at the figures below and write whether the figures are open or closed.

closed   open   open   closed   open

Write how many sides each polygon has on the lines below. Then write the name of the polygons.

8 sides   7 sides   5 sides
8 angles   5 angles   4 angles
octagon   arrow   polygon

Build Solid Foundations for Learning

Workbooks

Collections

Workpads

Flash Cards

Write & Wipes